AF575949

FIG. 1

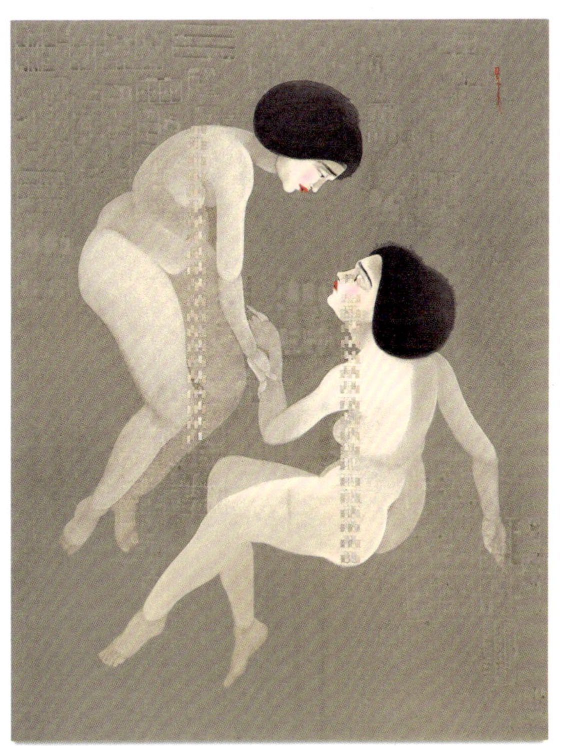

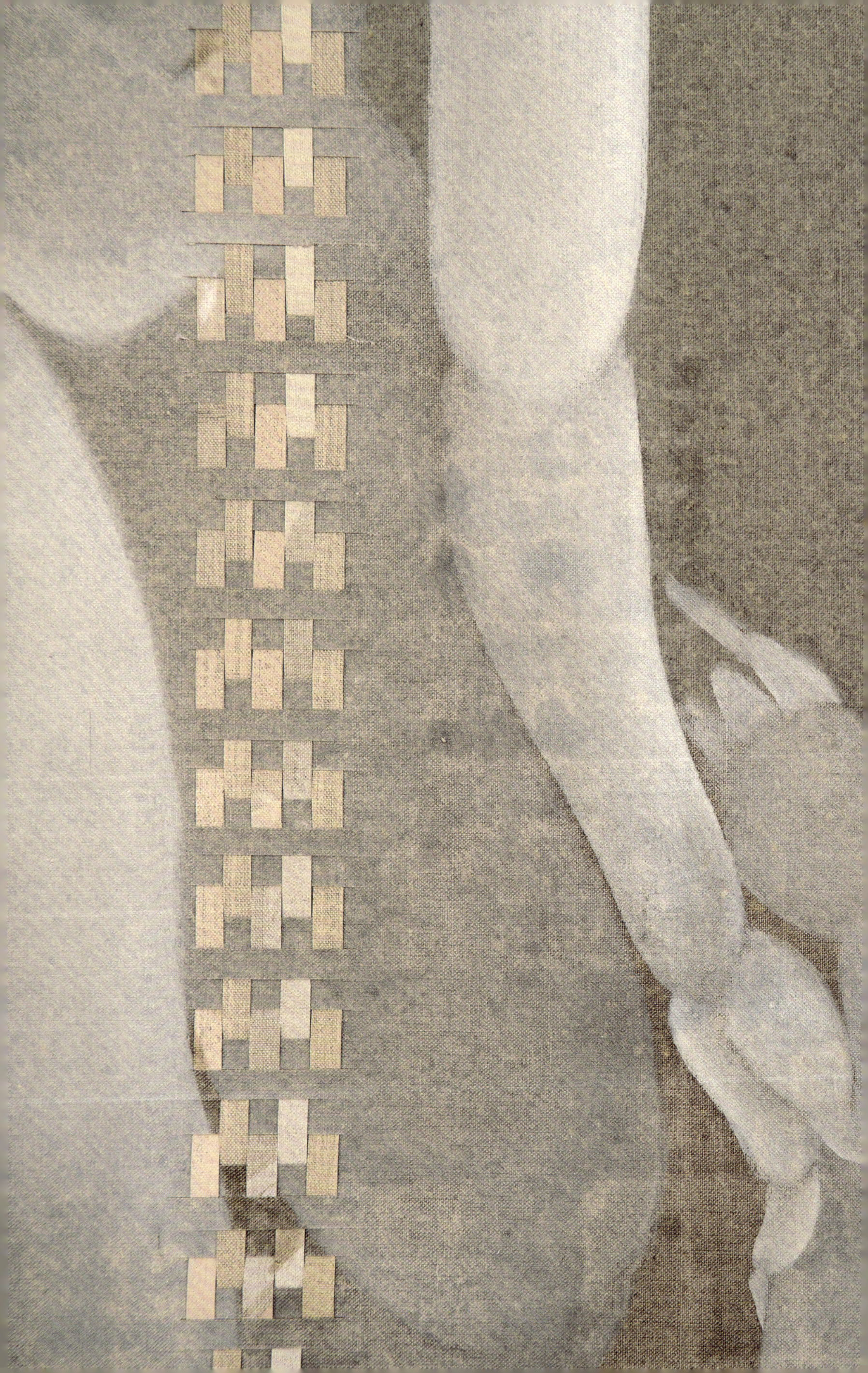

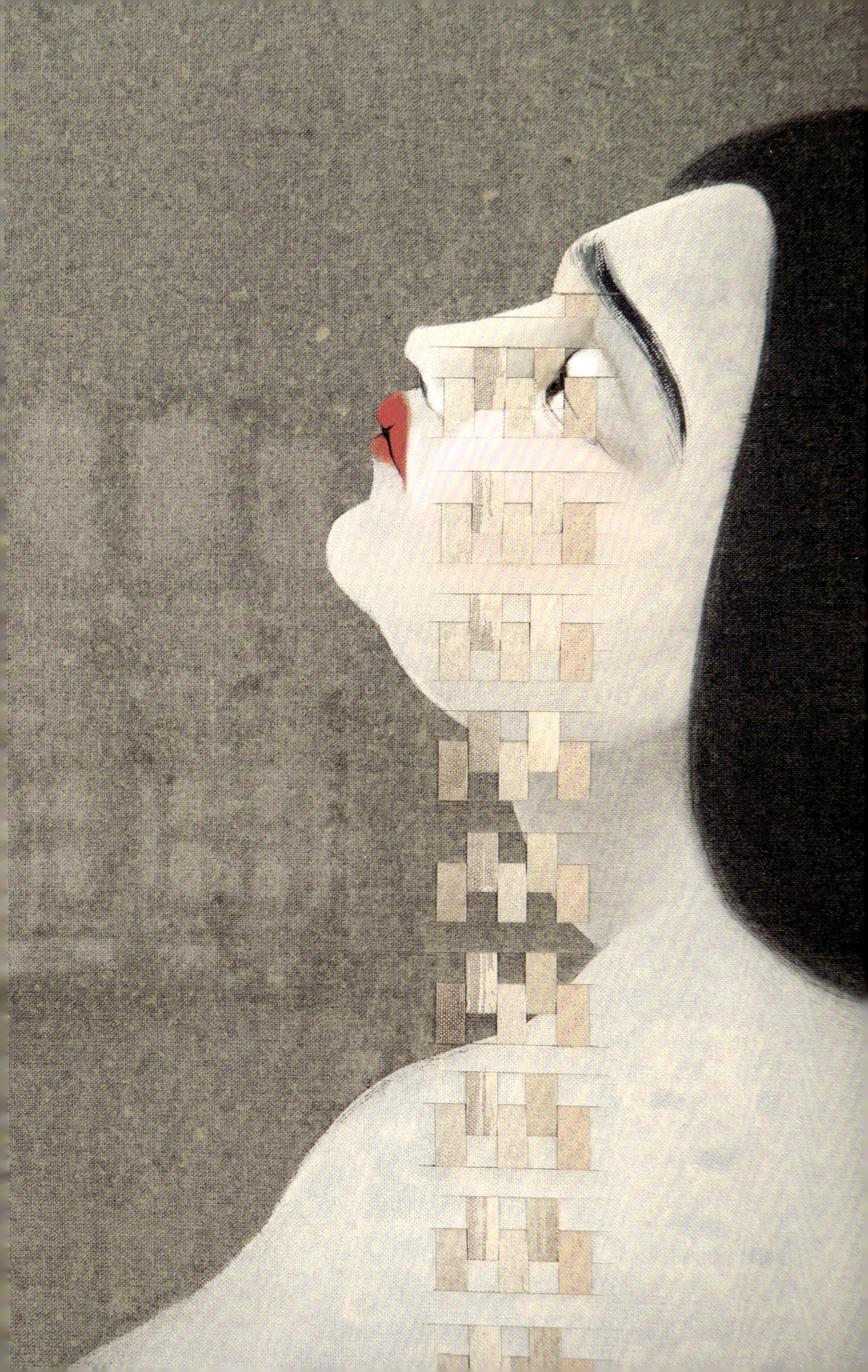

FIG. 2

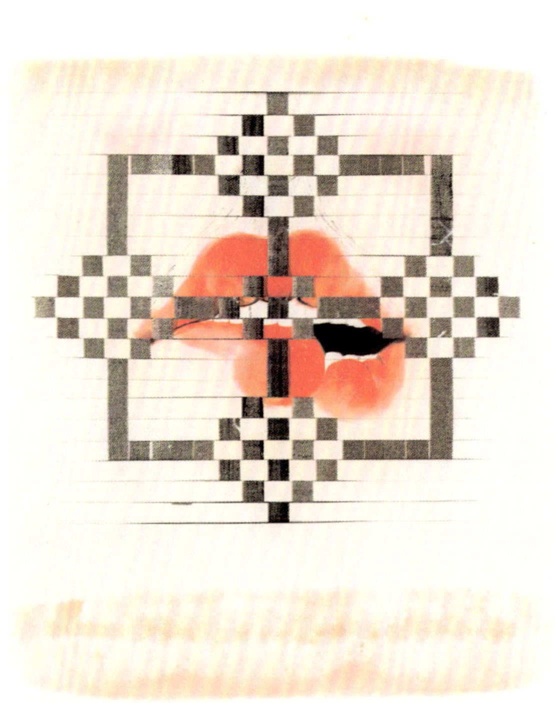

FIG. 2 (VERSO)

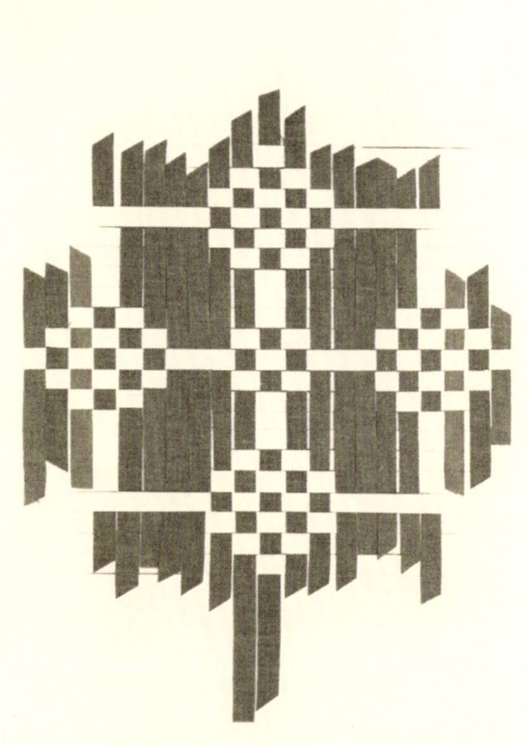

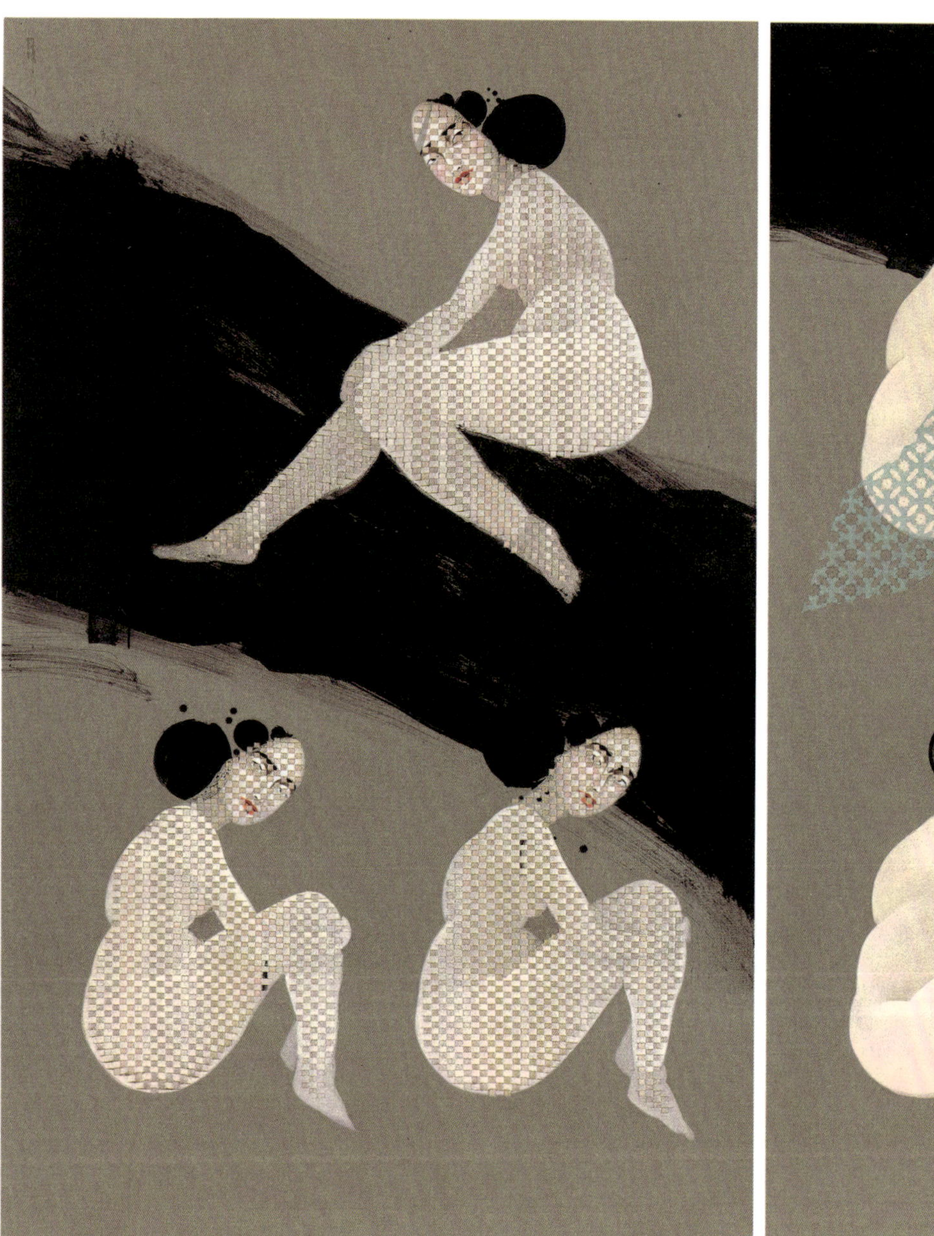

FIG. 3

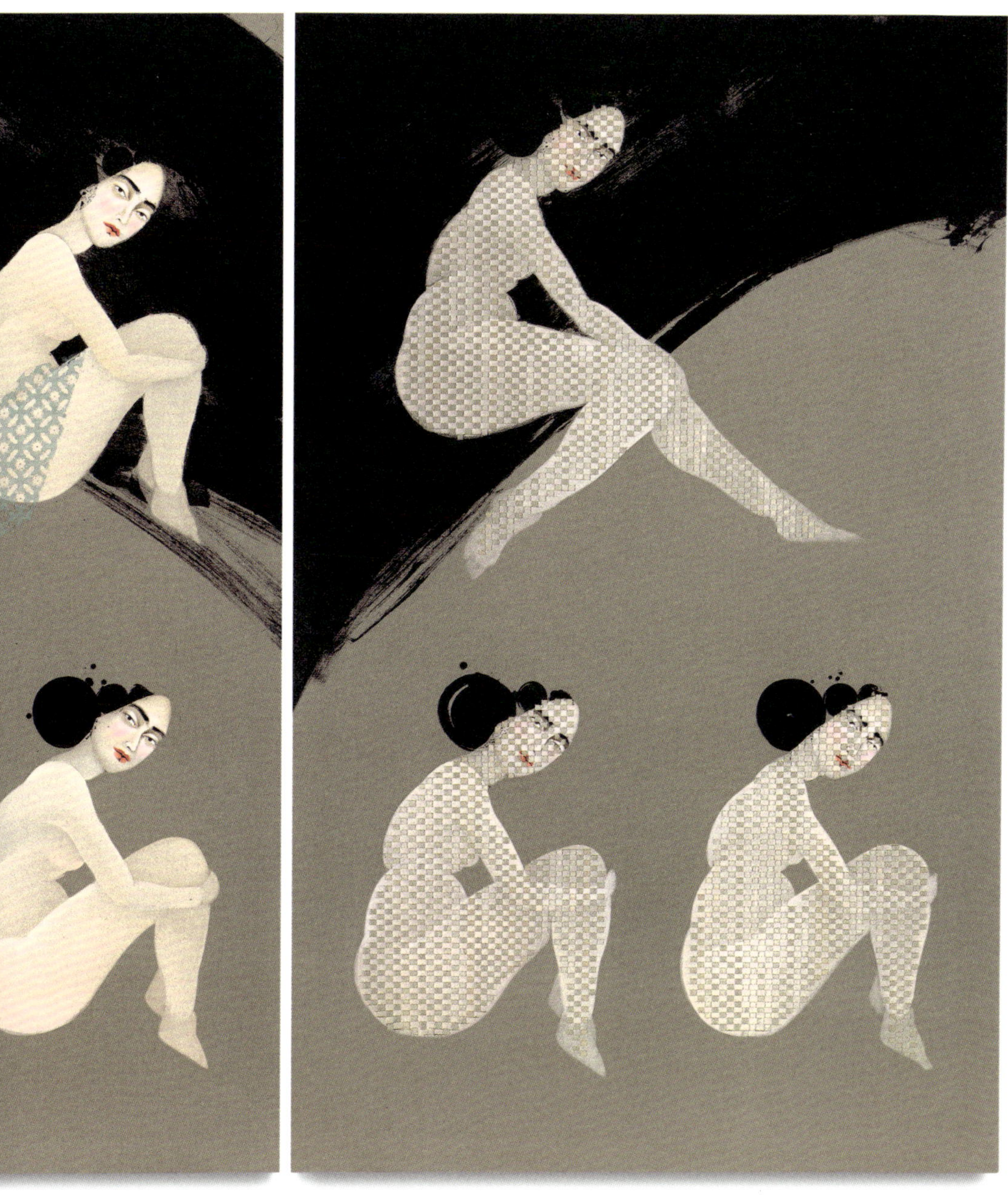

FIG. 3 (DETAIL)

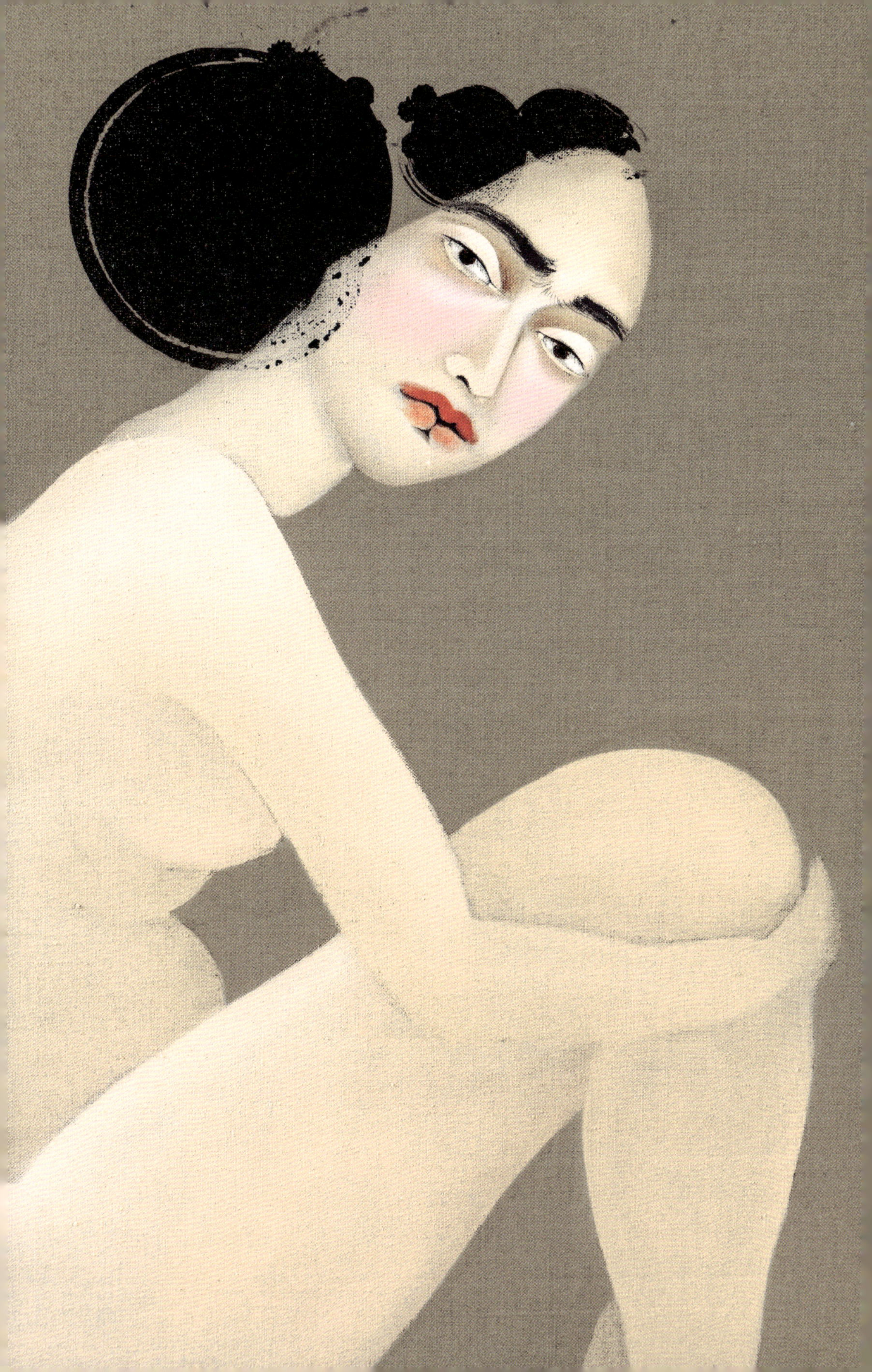

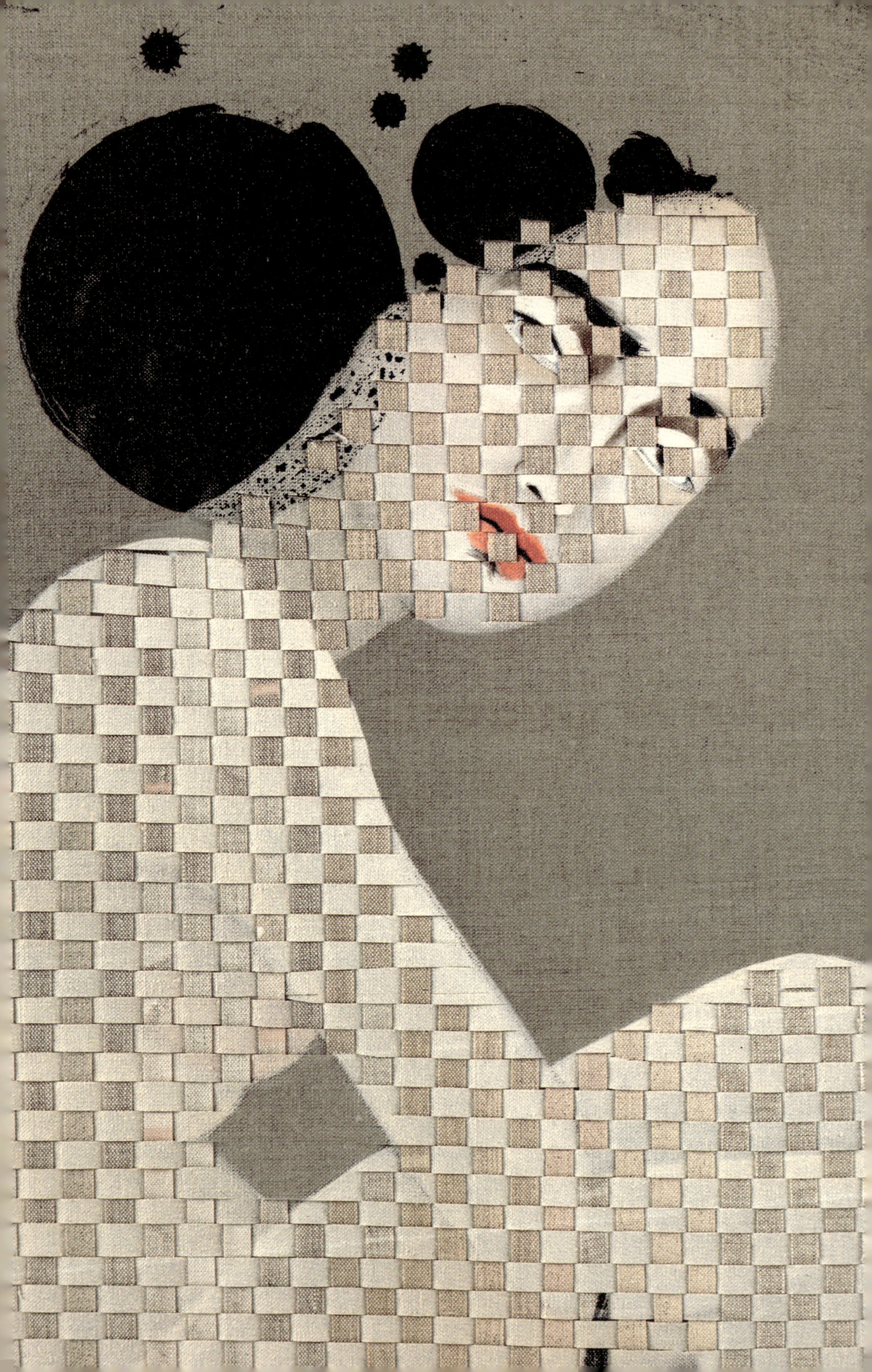

FIG. 3 (DETAIL)

FIG. 4

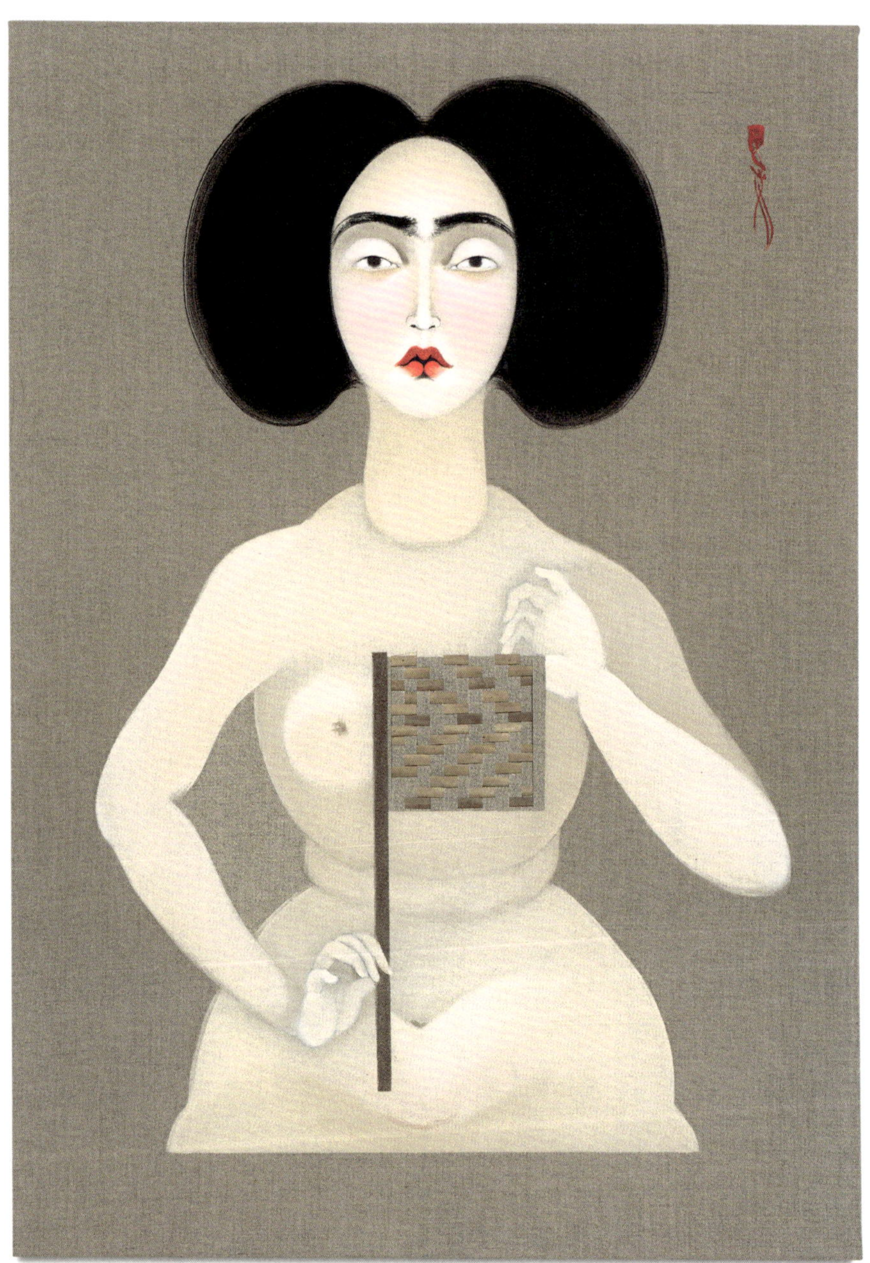

FIG. 5

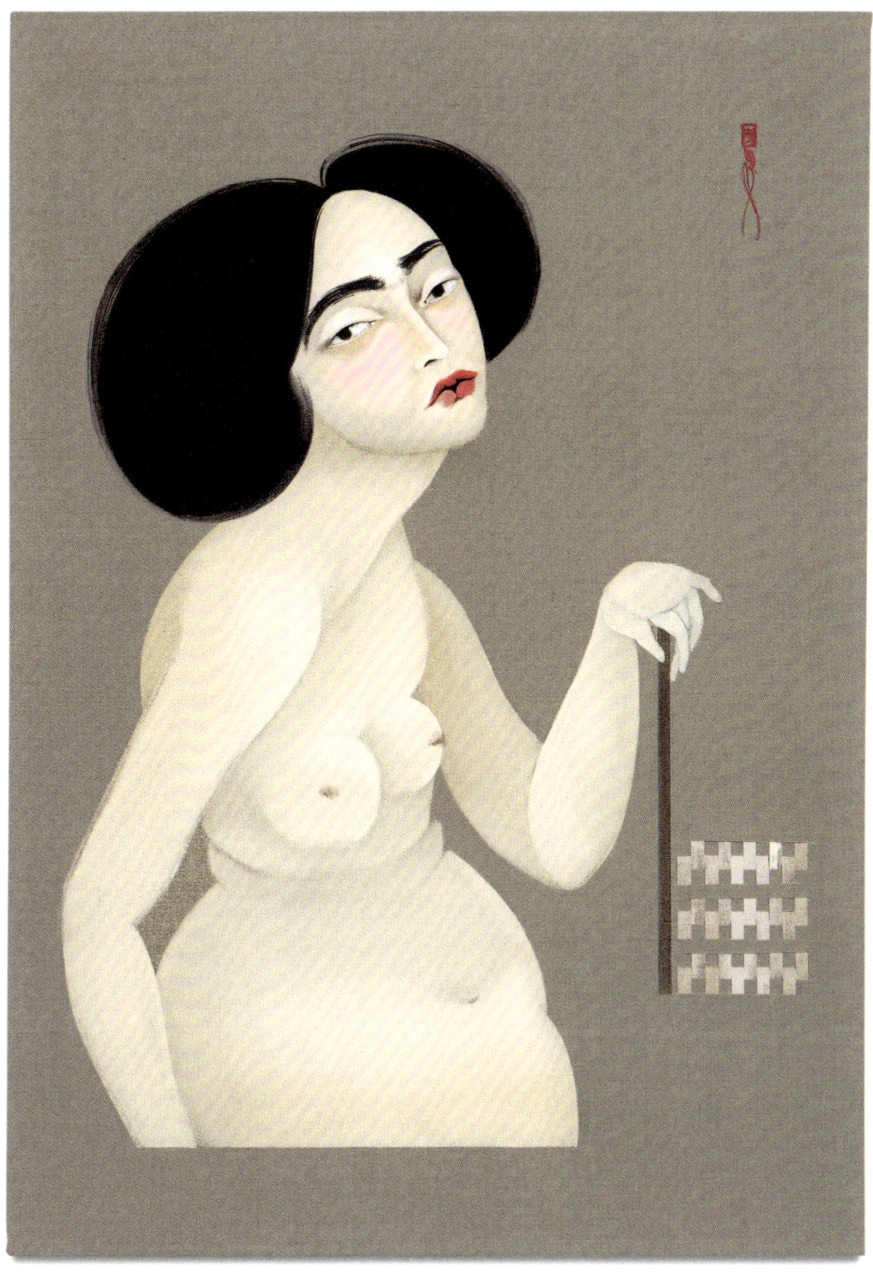

FIG. 6

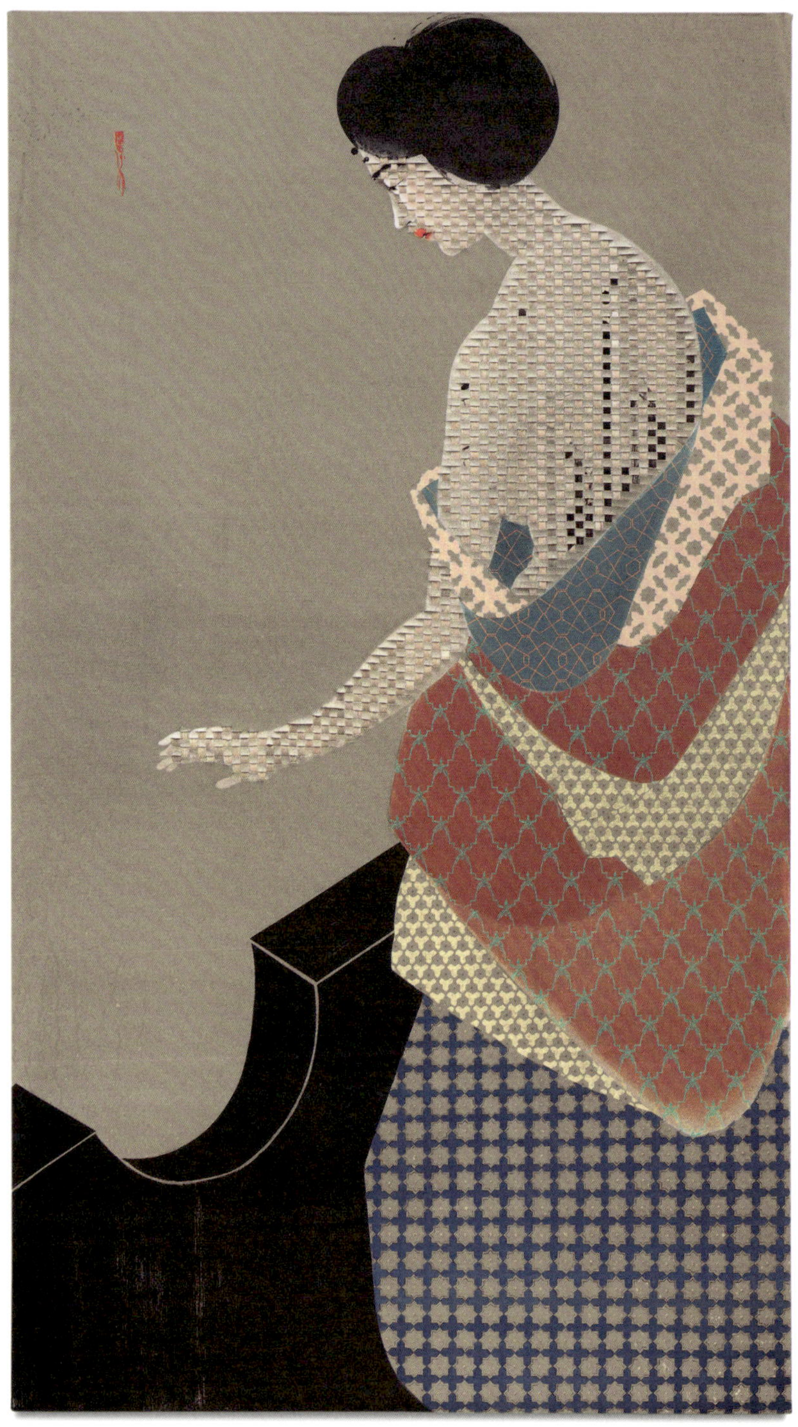

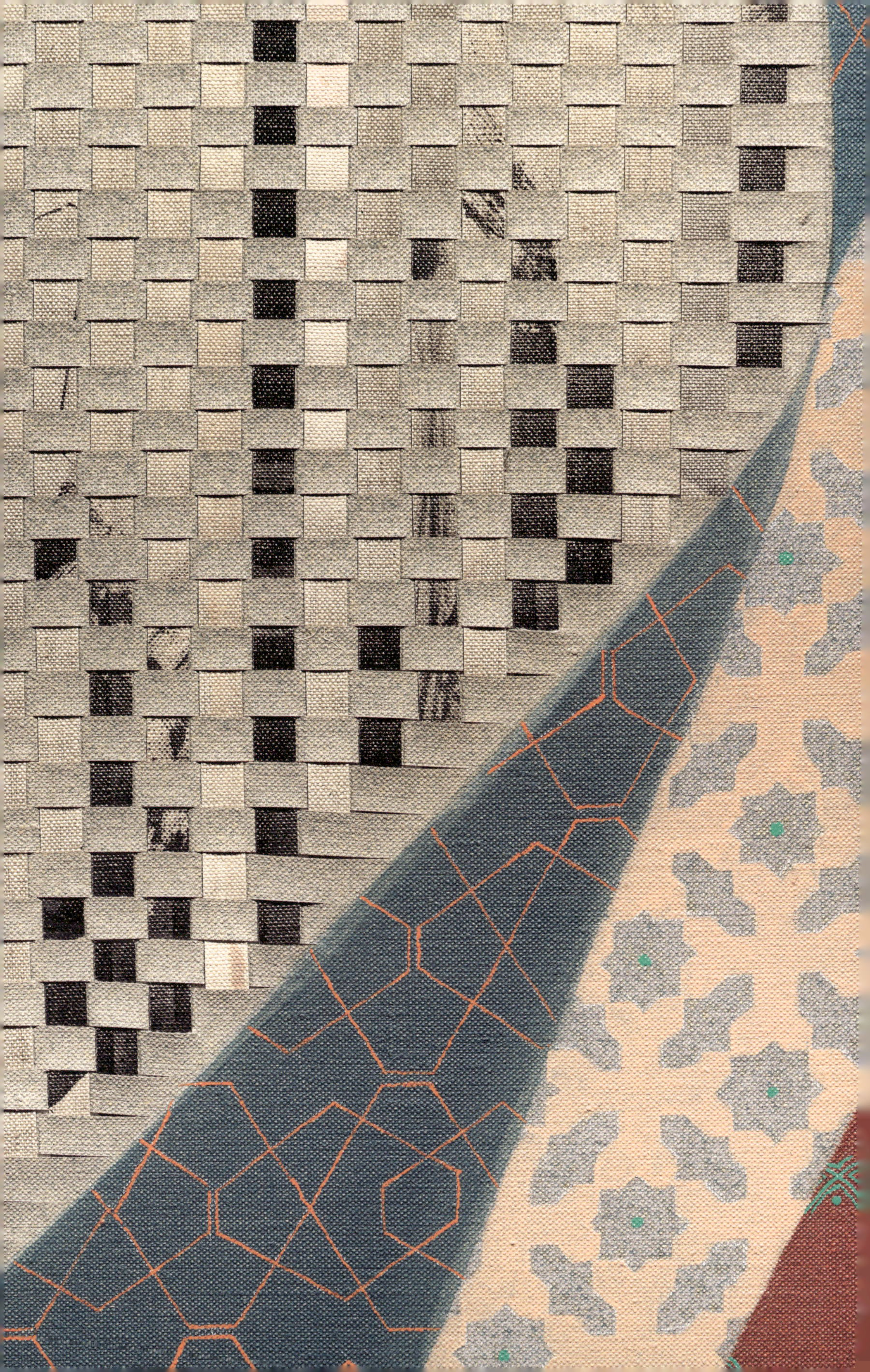

FIG. 7

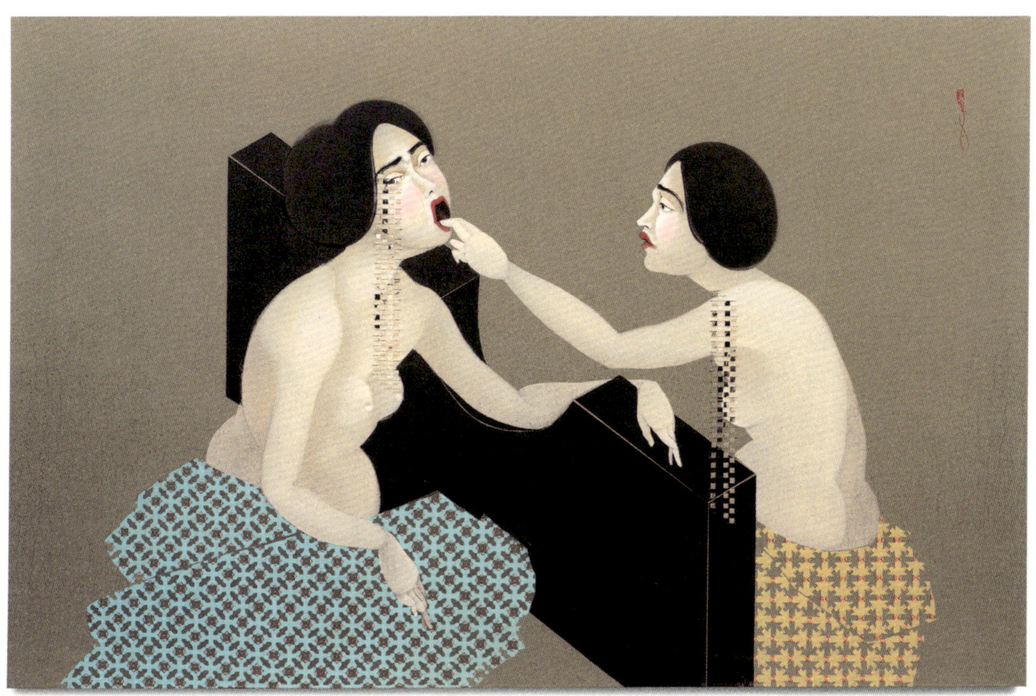

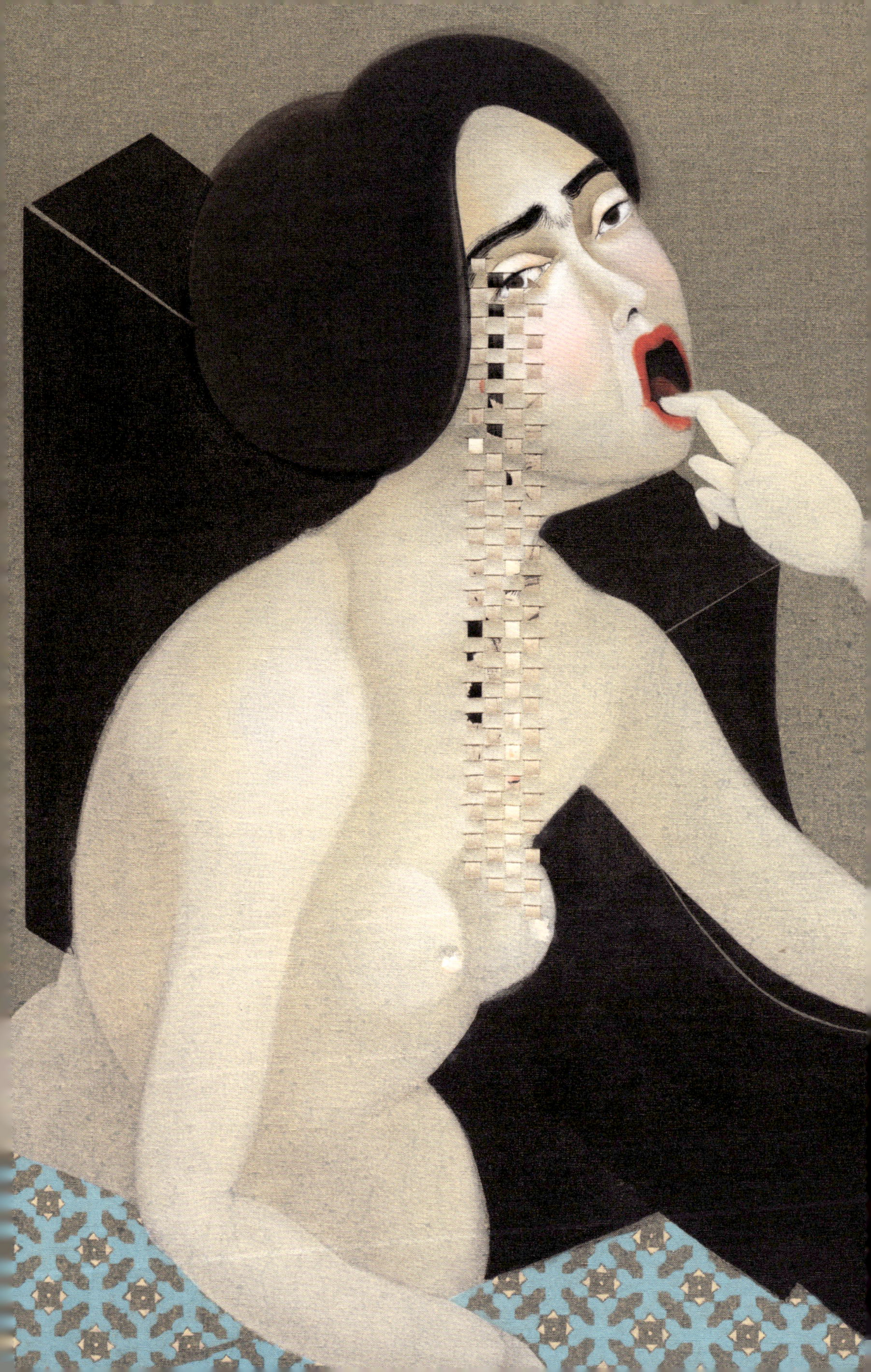

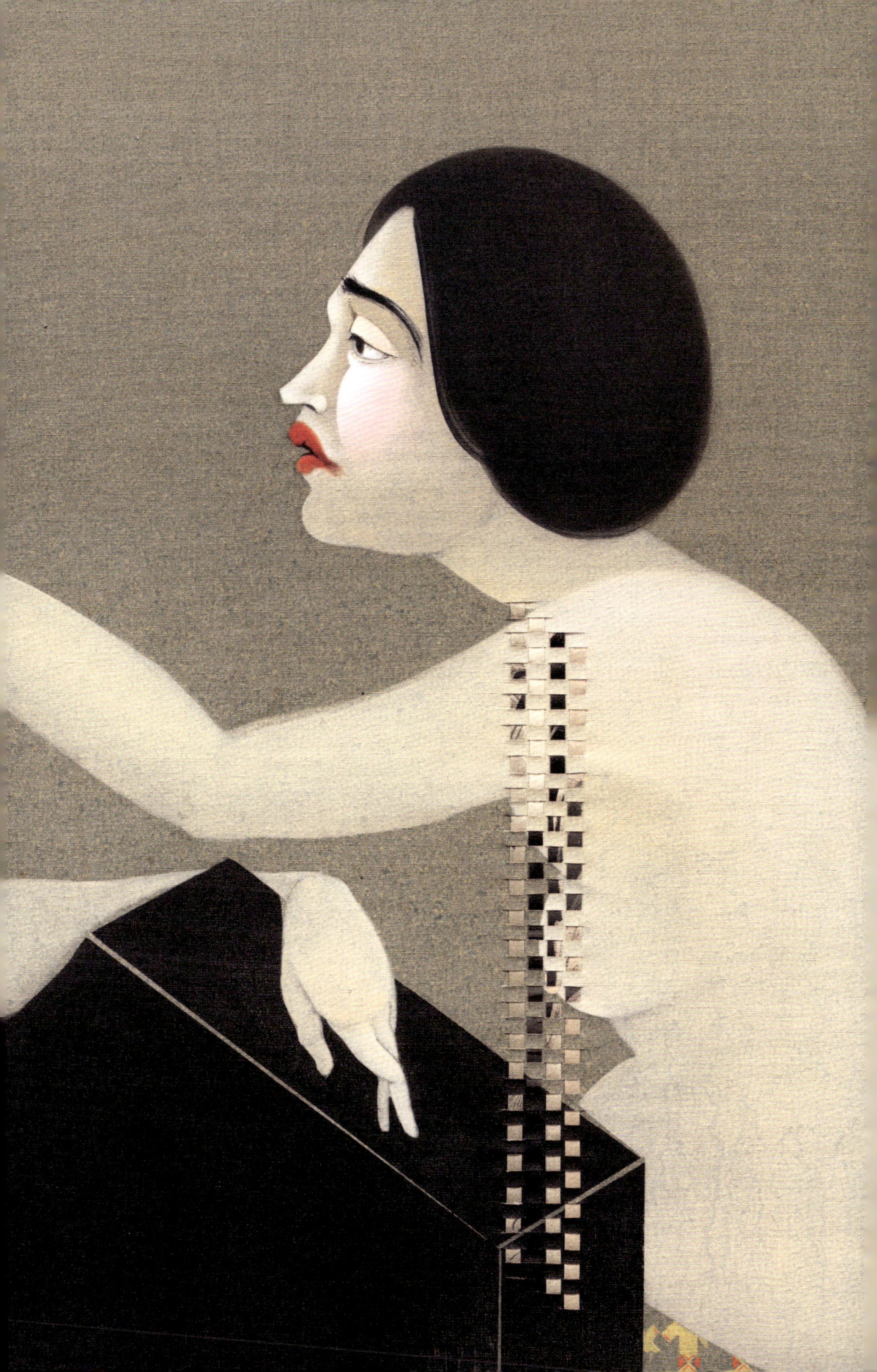

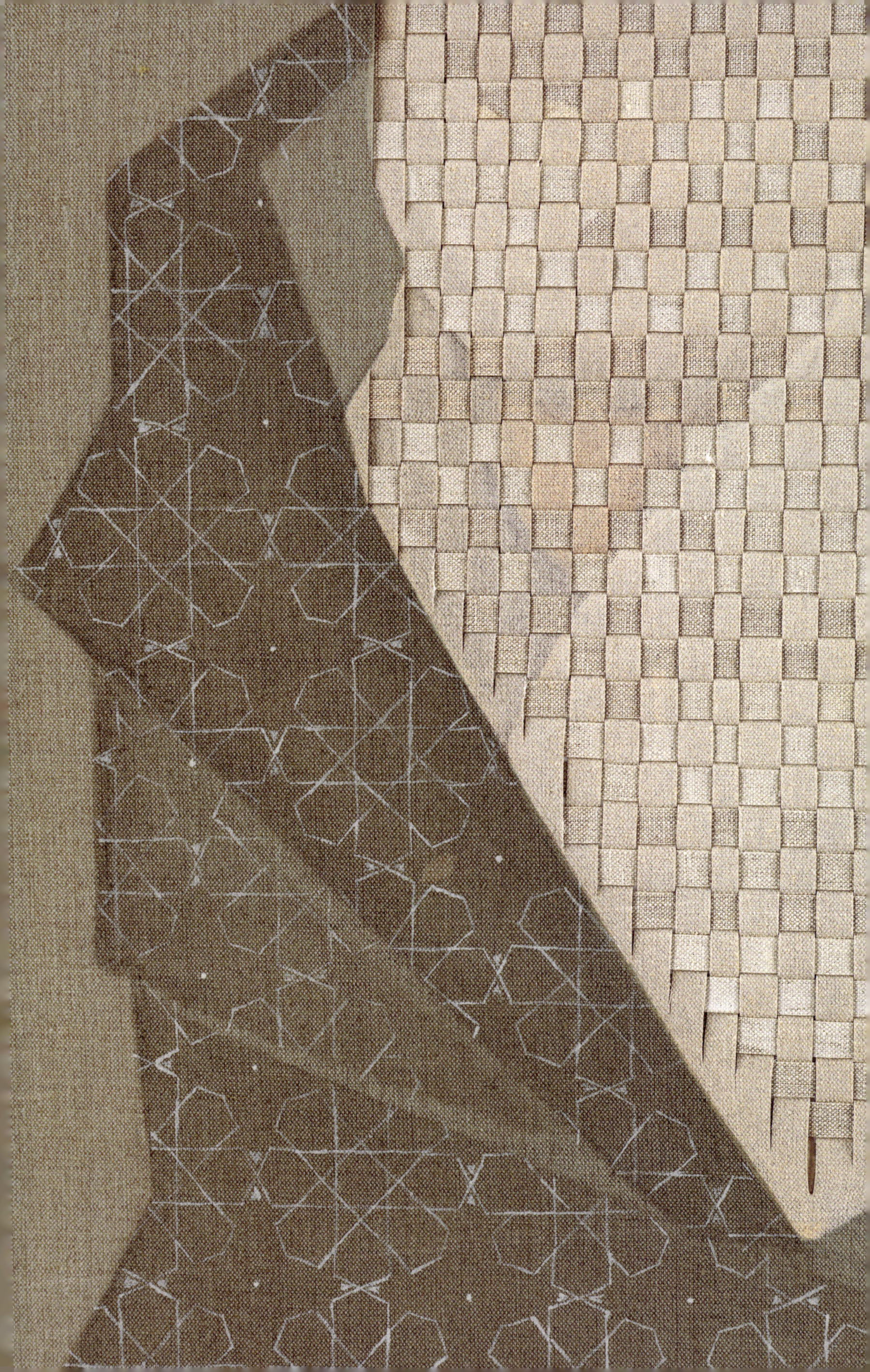

FIG. 8

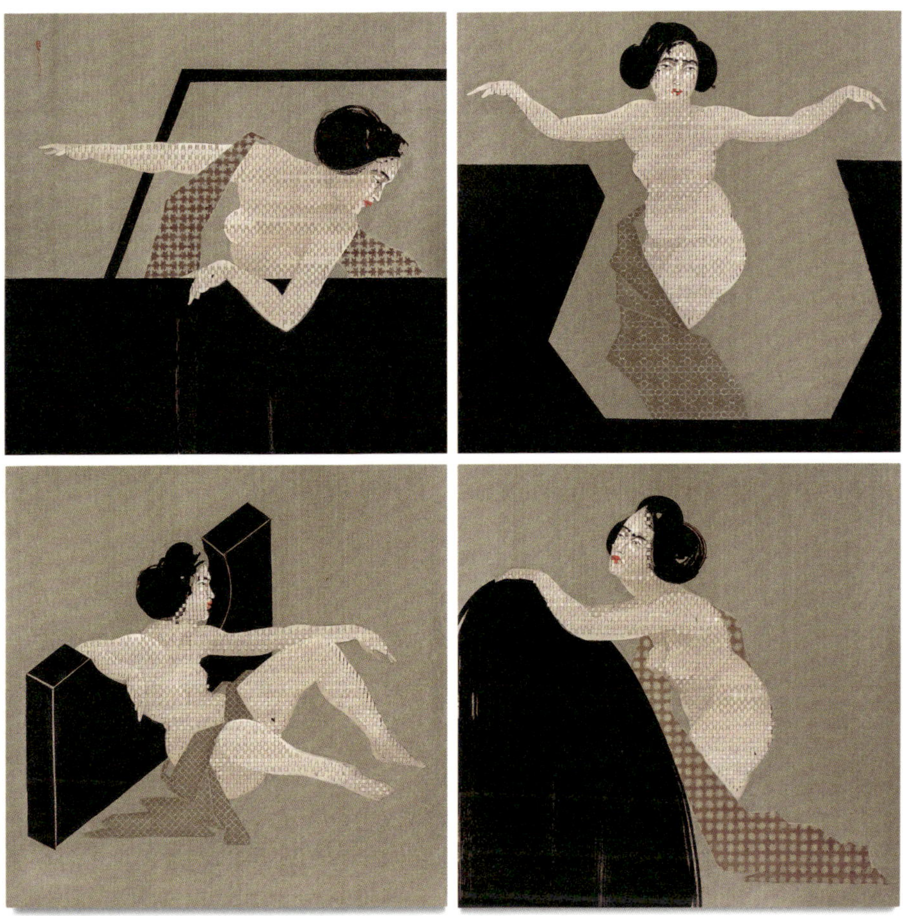

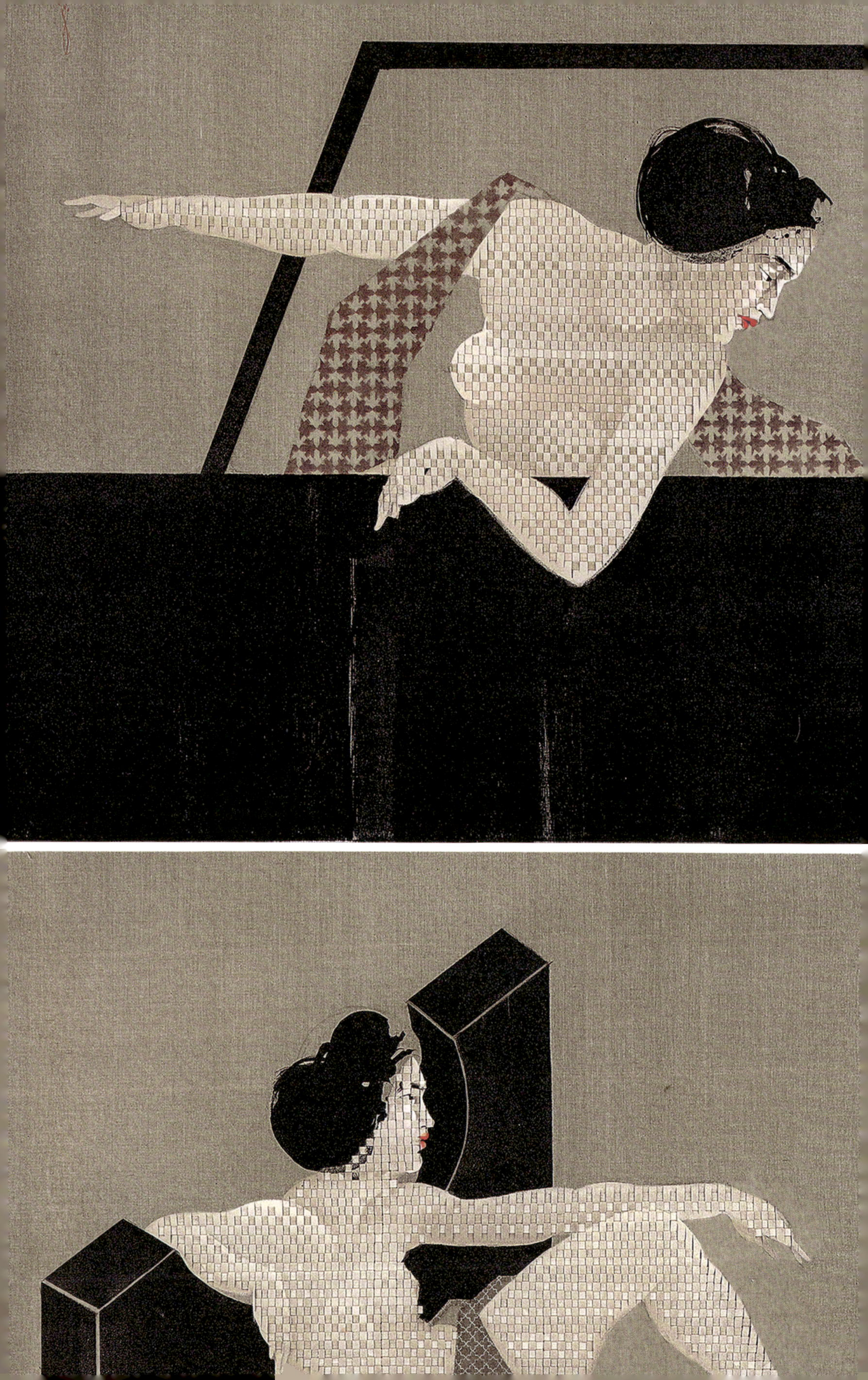

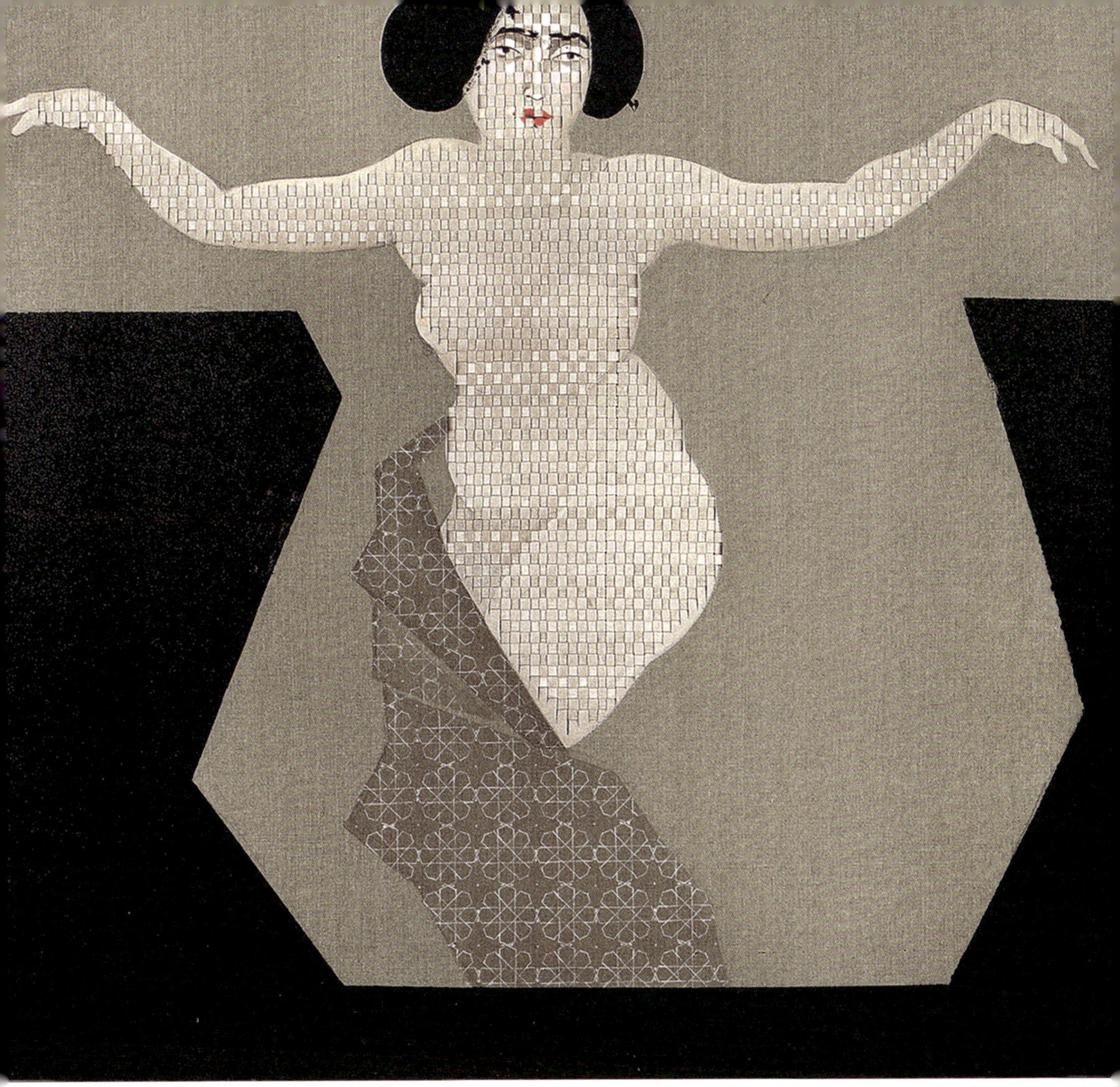

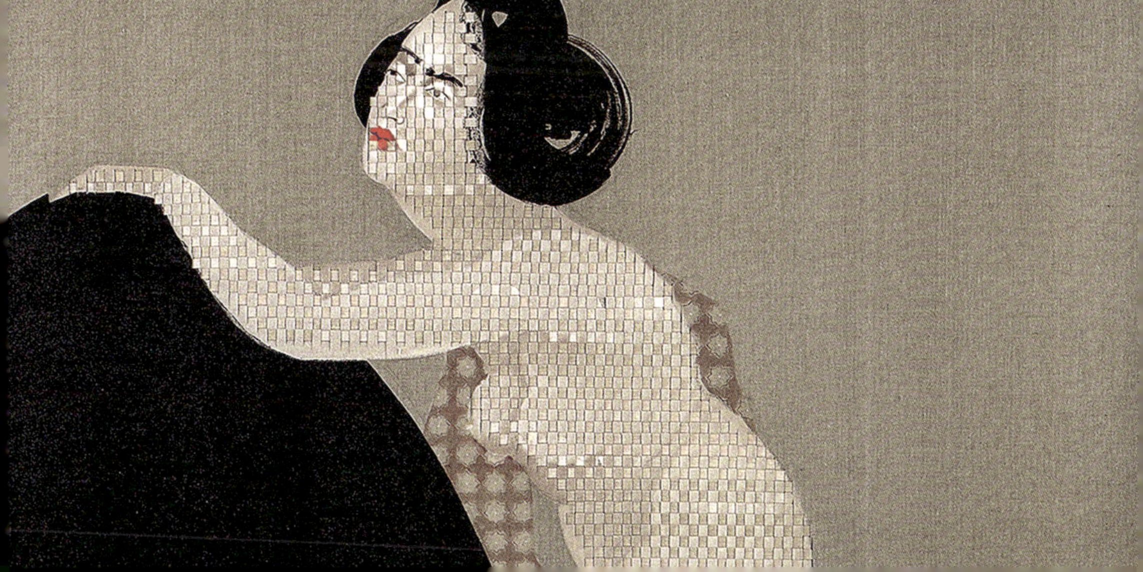

FIG. 9

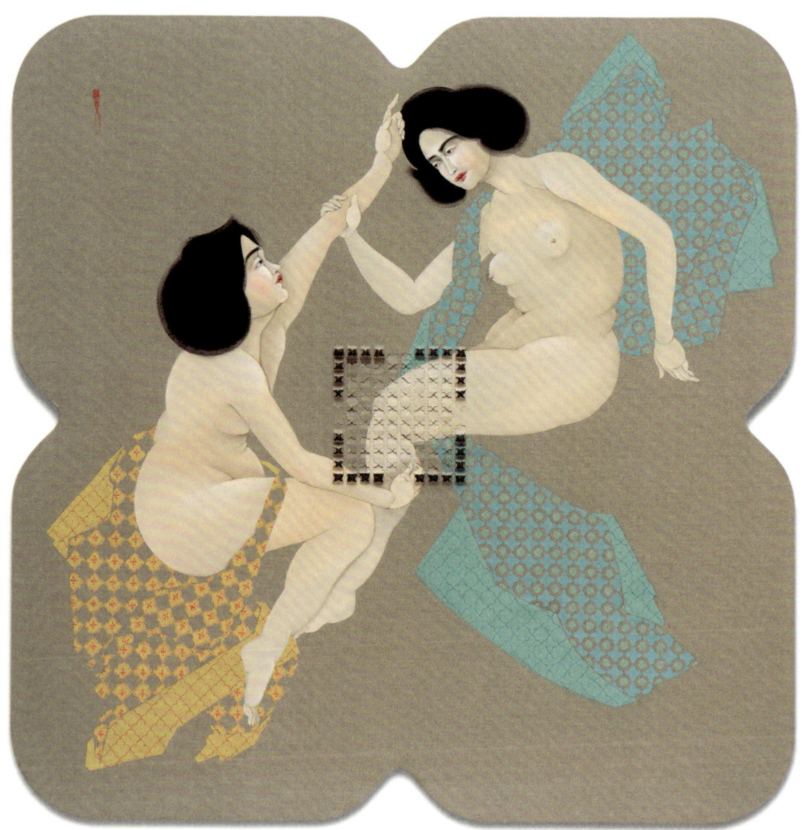

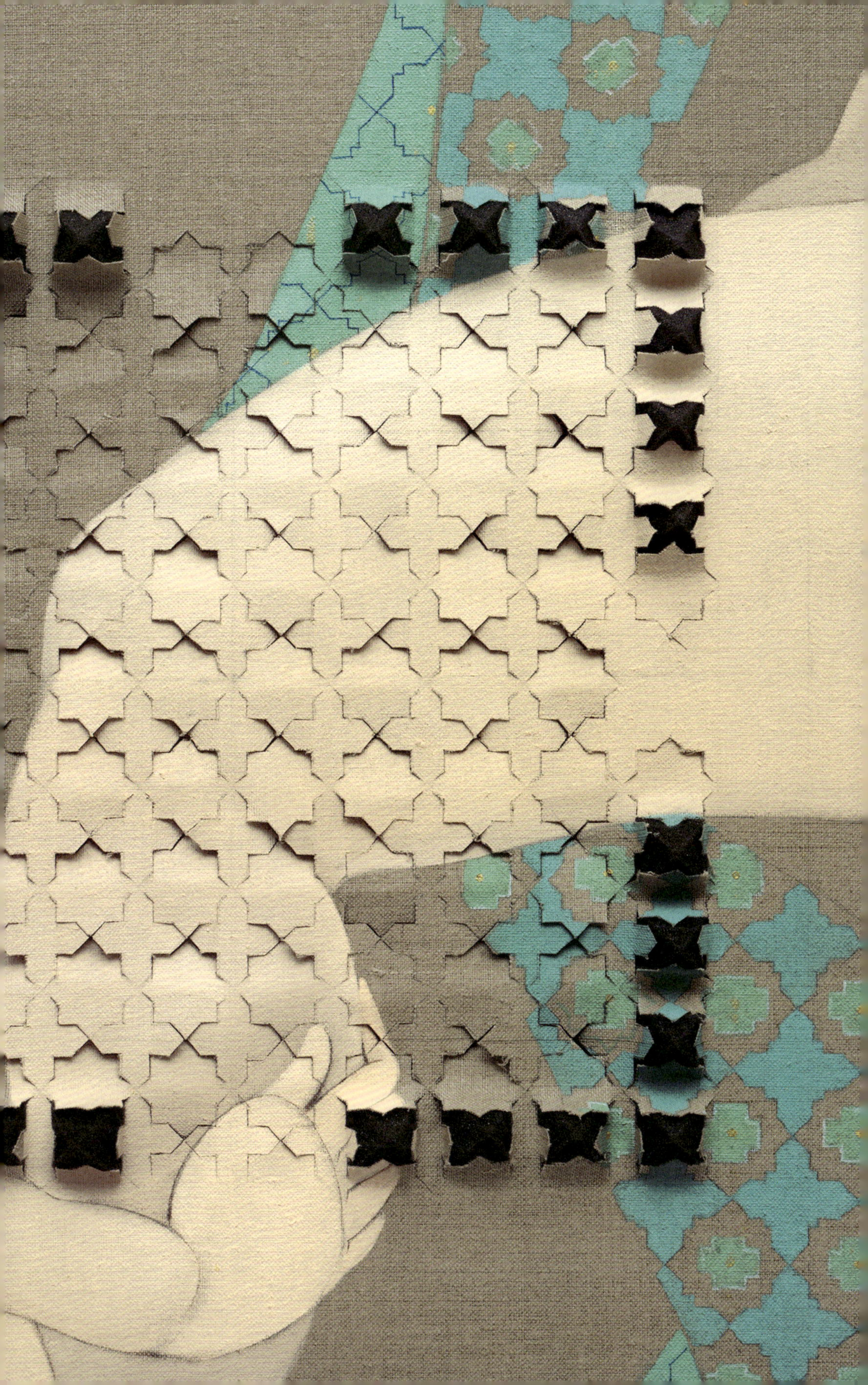

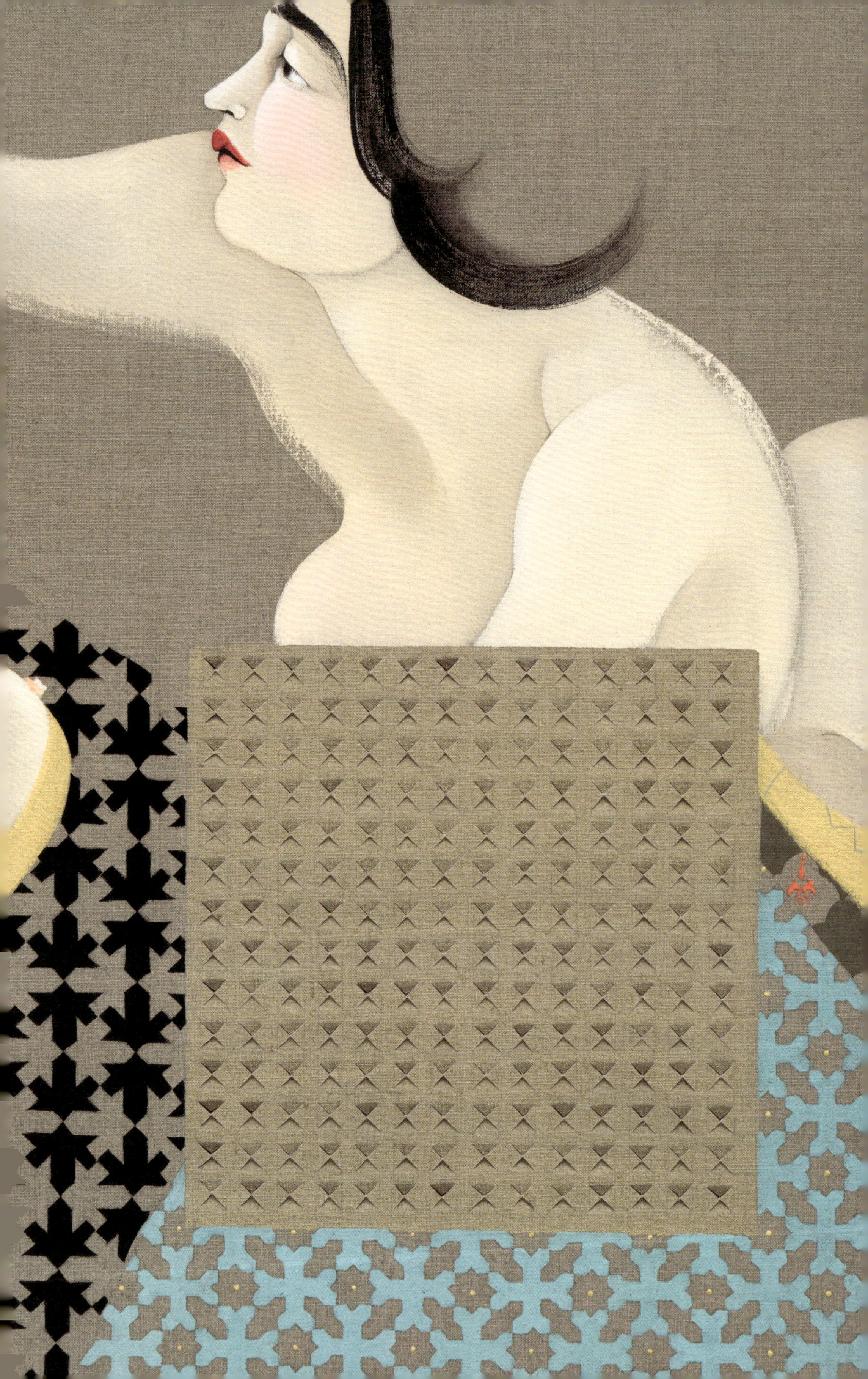

FIG. 10

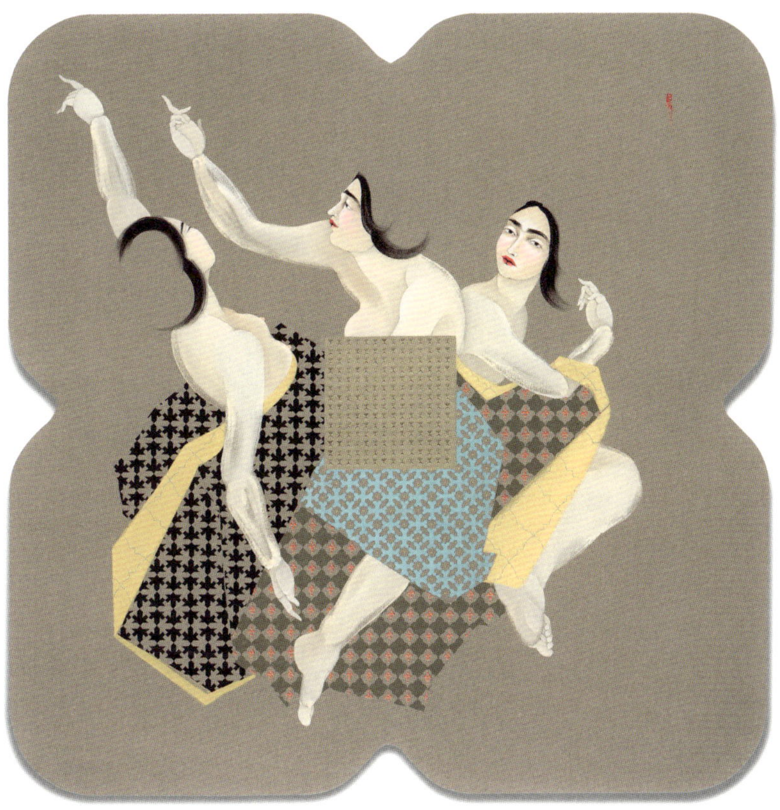

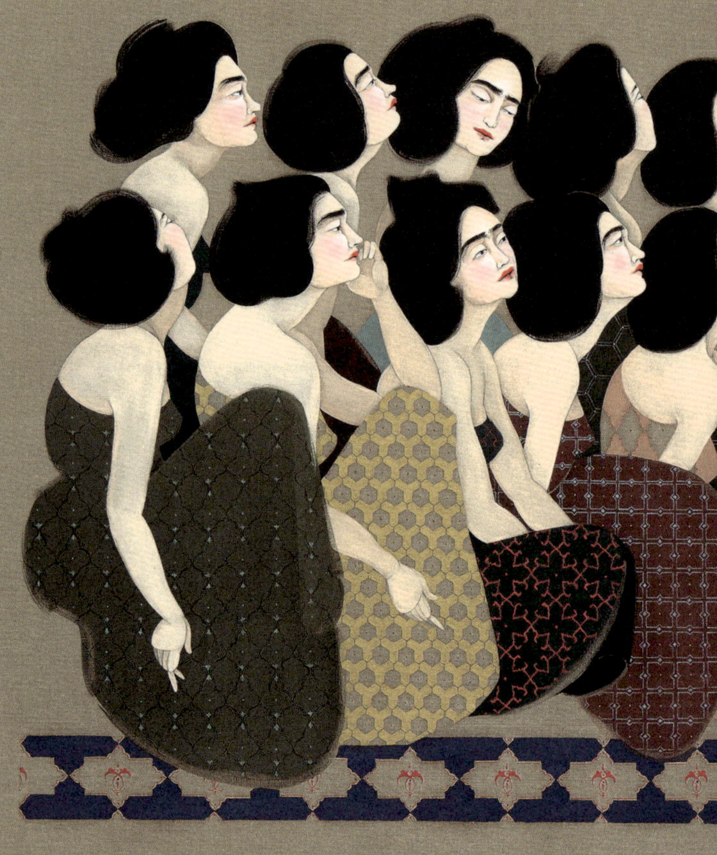
تهريب وتستخدم للدلالة على تهريب
ارج بلادهم عن طريق غير قانوني

FIG. 11

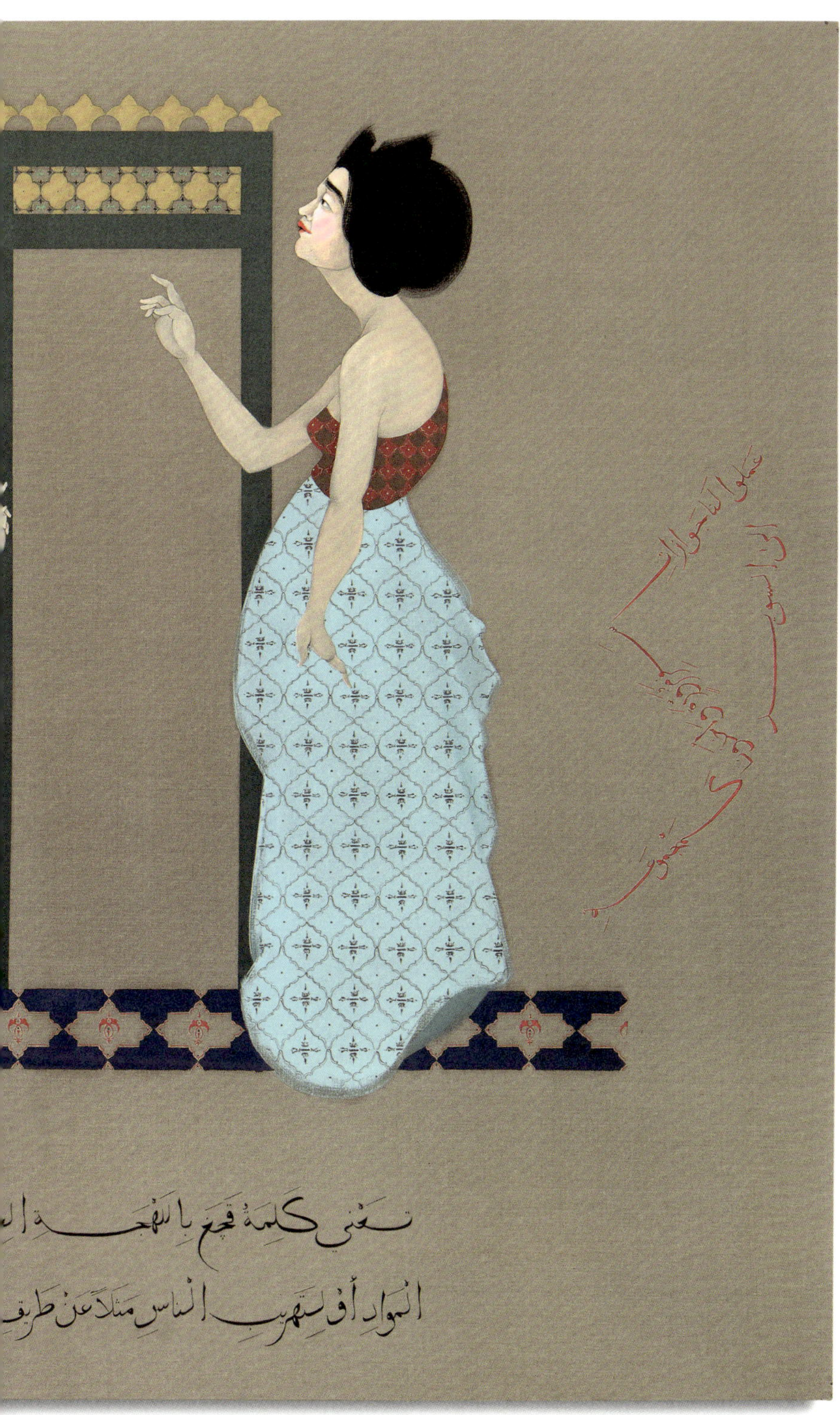

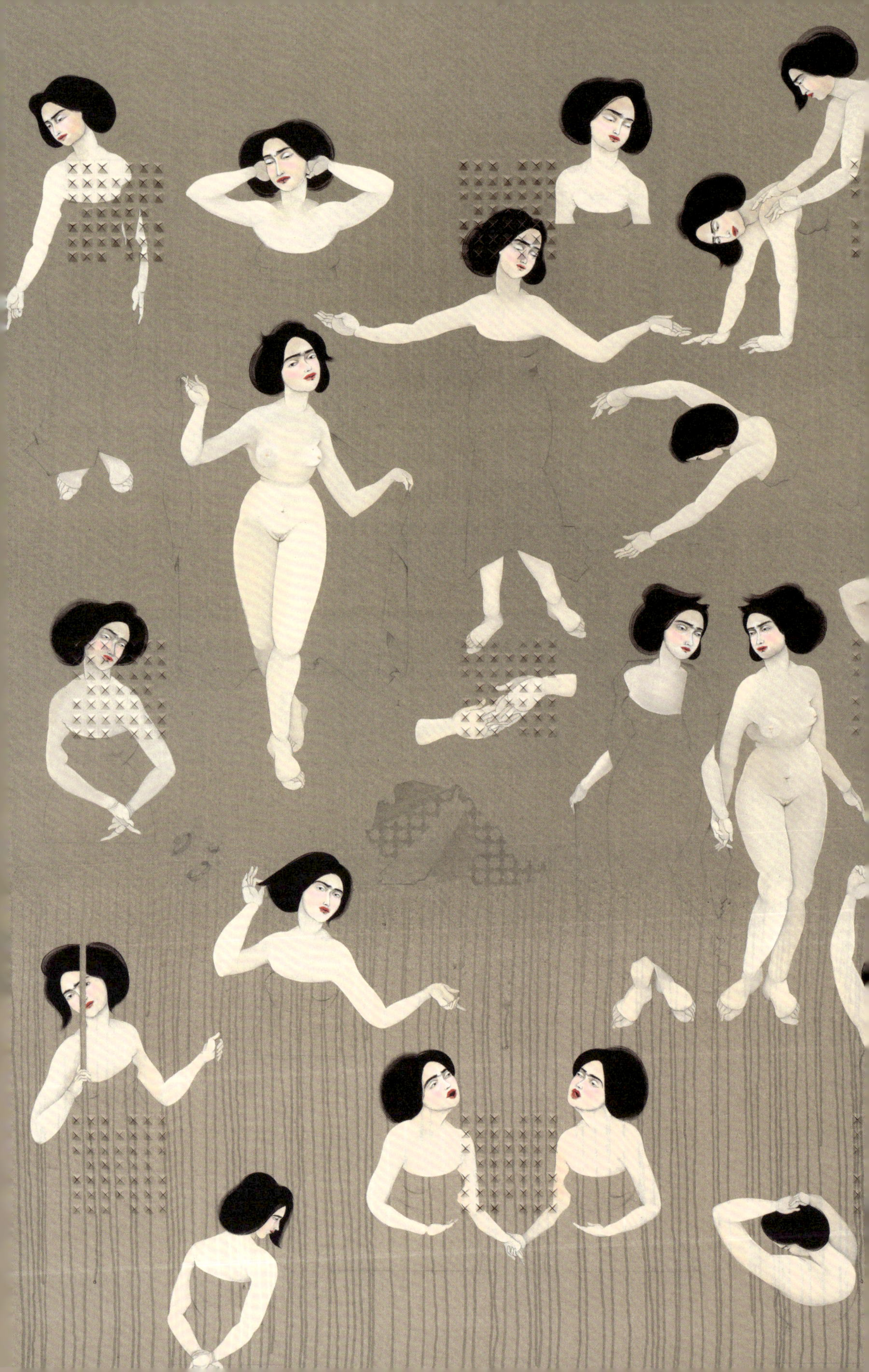

Hayv

Kahraman

Pomona College Museum of Art

List of Illustrations

fig. 1
Mnemonic Artifact 1, 2017
Oil on linen
70 × 54 in.
Private collection, New York
(detail on following spread)

fig. 2
Clock, 2017
Oil, linen, RSG, and pigment on paper
25 × 22¾ in.
(verso on following page)

fig. 3
Read me from right to left, 2017
Oil on linen triptych
78 × 150 in.
WASSART Collection, Switzerland
(details on following pages)

fig. 4
Mahaffa 1, 2017
Oil on linen
35 × 25 in.
Private collection, New York

fig. 5
Mahaffa 2, 2017
Oil on linen
35⅛ × 25⅛ in.
Private collection, Palo Alto, CA

fig. 6
Barricade 2, 2018
Oil on linen
70 × 40 in.
Pomona College Collection. Museum purchase made with funds provided by The Frederick Hammersley Foundation and the Dr. Louise M. Paris Fund
(detail on right)

fig. 7
Barricade 1, 2018
Oil on linen
50 × 78 in.
(detail on following spread)

fig. 8
Location of Attacker, 2017
Oil on linen quadriptych
100 × 96 in.
WASSART Collection, Switzerland
(details on left and following spread)

fig. 9
LRAD.1, 2016
Oil on linen and acoustic foam
64 × 64 in.
Private collection, Dublin, Ireland
(detail on right)

fig. 10
LRAD.3, 2016
Oil on linen and acoustic foam
64 × 64 in.
Private Collection, United Arab Emirates
(detail on left)

fig. 11
Kachakchi, 2015
Oil on linen
79 × 108 in.
Collection of Bill and Christy Gautreaux, Kansas City, MO

fig. 12
Search, 2016
Oil on linen
96 × 73 in.
Los Angeles County Museum of Art (LACMA), Los Angeles
(detail)

Hayv

Kahraman

Edited by—
Rebecca McGrew

Contributions by—
Sinan Antoon
Hayv Kahraman
Madina Tlostanova

Project Series 52

Contents

Introduction—
Hayv Kahraman: Weaving as Mending

Rebecca McGrew

In Los Angeles-based artist Hayv Kahraman's twelve-foot long painting, *Read me from right to left* (2017) [fig. 3], ten ghostly, almost identical, nude women sit immobile in two rows, arms wrapped around their legs, somberly gazing at the viewer. The exquisitely painted figures, each with iridescent pale skin and inky black circles of abstracted hair, float enigmatically on the triptych's linen surface, which is bifurcated by massive black slashes of brushed oil paint. Scars composed of interwoven strips of shredded paintings mark some of the women's bodies, echoing the Islamic geometric patterns on the pale blue shawls draped over two women's laps.

For Kahraman, these ten female bodies—like the female bodies in her other paintings—represent *She*: "someone who dwells in the margins, surviving and navigating a life of spatial and temporal displacement . . . *She* lives in the now that is tainted by a ghostly yesterday."[1] Kahraman's paintings tackle themes of violence and involuntary migration as she processes her childhood in war-torn Iraq and her adolescence in Sweden as a refugee. While Kahraman's work is intertwined with the harrowing histories of the Iran-Iraq and Gulf Wars, it is also invested in the idea of feminine collectivity, identity, belonging, and diasporic cultural memory.

For over a decade, Kahraman has explored painting as protest and reckoning in works that are formally elegant and skillfully painted depictions of the compulsively repeated *She*. The artist borrows from a multiplicity of styles—including Persian miniatures, Japanese woodcuts, and Italian Renaissance paintings—in the composition of the woman's poses and appearance, creating a discourse between Eastern "otherness" and Western concepts of beauty. Absorbing Renaissance aesthetic values while simultaneously rejecting hegemonic ideals, Kahraman models the bodies in her paintings on representations of her own body. She photographs herself in poses, assuming multiple personas, that she then sketches in paint onto the brown linen panels. The artist considers this process a performative act that heals by repeatedly reexamining her history.

1. Kahraman, in "The Art of Mending," *Acts of Reparation: Hayv Kahraman* (St. Louis, MO: Contemporary Art Museum, St. Louis, 2017) 15–16, discusses who *She* is and where she came from, citing a formative time in her early twenties, when, as a student of graphic design in Italy, she spent hours in museums in Florence, Italy, studying Renaissance painting. Kahraman ultimately discovered that *She* was the embodiment of someone who was colonized.

Each new body of work stems from a mnemonic incident as a catalyst. For example, *Read me from right to left* originated when a traumatic childhood memory resurfaced at the outset of the 2017 travel ban. Kahraman remembered being forced to remain immobile during her flight from Baghdad in 1992. A visual protest to the ban, the painting contrasts English and Arabic—in Arabic you read from right to left. Kahraman suggests that "reading" the situation differently offers the opportunity to consider anew migrant consciousness and experience. Kahraman's memories of trauma are embodied in her female figures as "fractured, multisensory pulsations of the past, present, and future."[2]

2. Hayv Kahraman, email to author, August 23, 2017.

In earlier series, Kahraman has portrayed women engaging in harmful beauty rituals (the series "Pins and Needles," 2010), and contorting their bodies into unnatural poses based on U.S. military translation cards (the series "Audible Inaudible," 2016). While the figure Kahraman repeatedly paints represents herself as a colonized diasporic woman, it also stands in for others caught in the trauma of war and conflict or oppressed due to their gender or race who must relive their own visceral memories of horrific violence.

Echoing the psychic and physical wounds the refugee/migrant experiences over time and geography, the "Audible Inaudible" series of paintings marked the moment Kahraman first began ripping or puncturing her canvases. In more recent work, including *Read me from right to left,* Kahraman has incorporated a weaving technique drawn from the Iraqi hand-woven fans called *mahaffa*, one of the few family heirlooms she possesses. She cuts into her canvases—her painted body—and then weaves in fragments of other shredded or dismembered paintings, creating newly "mended" representations of female bodies and "healed" memories of past trauma. Through the bodies of these women, the repetitive nature of her work, and the act of shredding and mending, Kahraman grapples with a history of displacement, loss, memory, and trauma.

This publication highlights her artistic process of shredding as undoing and weaving as repairing. It makes Kahraman's nuanced transtemporal and transcultural perspectives apparent. Kahraman and graphic designer Kimberly Varella engage these complicated threads in an artistic collaboration resulting in *Hayv Kahraman,* a hybrid artist book and exhibition catalog. Photographs from the artist's studio are interwoven with intimate texts, literally emulating and evoking the core processes and themes of Kahraman's works. This book includes the full text of

Kahraman's autobiographical performance script, which elucidates how her often painful experiences and memories merge with her artwork's evolution towards a more whole tapestry of future possibilities.

Catalog essayist Madina Tlostanova's prior scholarship eloquently synthesizes the impetus of Kahraman's works: "the decolonial tempo-localities are often recreated through rituals of remembering and reconstruction, through efforts to extract the spatial memory, through merging with space, through physical and bodily amalgamating in the palimpsest of many contradictory cultural layers, historical events, and natural landscapes."[3] Tlostanova expands this exploration in her essay in this book, navigating how Kahraman's work, in processing her trauma, heals both her self and her world anew. Writer, poet, and scholar Sinan Antoon's two new poems in this volume painfully, yet beautifully, suggest how Kahraman's work "arrives bearing visible and invisible scars and carrying the weight of history and its injuries and traumas" and becomes "the painful embodiment of memory."[4] By bringing together Kahraman's mnemonic paintings and her personal writing with Antoon's English and Arabic poetry and Tlostanova's incisive analysis of Kahraman's practice, this volume, in its very existence, echoes Kahraman's desire for her work and her memories to become "a bridge to the past life and a way to sustain the future."[5]

3.
Madina Tlostanova, *Postcolonialism & Postsocialism in Fiction and Art: Resistance and Re-existance* (Cham, Switzerland: Palgrave Macmillan, 2017), 101.

4.
Sinan Antoon, "Re-membering the Present and Unpacking Memory," 2017. Essay for Jack Shaiman Gallery exhibition.

5.
Kahraman, email to author, August 23, 2017.

Re-weaving one's world anew—Hayv Kahraman and the art of re-existence

Madina Tlostanova

> **Life is a perpetual to and fro, a dis/continuous releasing and absorbing of the self. Let her weave her story within their stories, her life amidst their lives. And while she weaves, let her whip, spur, and set them on fire. Thus making them sing again. Very softly a-new, a-gain.**
> **—Trinh T. Minh-ha[1]**

Hayv Kahraman's deeply disturbing and, at the same time, cathartic works have fascinated me from the very first encounter. They open a path to a decolonial "community of sense," a paradoxical mixture of rational and emotional responses, analytical approaches, and specific optics. This community of sense links different experiences marked by global coloniality—a full dependence on models of thinking, seeing, and interpreting the world on the norms created and imposed by/in the Western modernity.[2] The haunting images of *She*—the artist's alter ego—trigger decolonial solidarity through sadness, indignation, hope, and resolution to restore the right to be different. In Kahraman's case, coloniality looms in its cruelest form of the deprivation of dignity and the negation of human life as such. The artist communicates the feeling of exclusion and non-being that so many of the translated and transplanted individuals share and at the same time, the powerful impulse of remaking oneself anew and overcoming the limitations of the human condition, marked by coloniality. Her art creolizes various traditions, decenters aesthetic canons, and delinks from legitimized ways of perception.

On top of our shared sensibility of multiple border selves, I was also looking for a more personal entry point into Kahraman's art that would connect our two different local histories and personal narratives of displaced and "unhomed"[3] people. This entry point had to be emotional, even visceral—to be able to trigger the decolonial sublime as a way of transcending the global coloniality through correlating one's personal experience of being objectified, erased, or exoticized with other manifestations of the darker side of modernity and with other ways of resisting.

1. Trinh T. Minh-ha, *Woman, Native, Other: Writing Postcoloniality and Feminism* (Bloomington, IN and Indianapolis: Indiana University Press, 1986), 128.

2. Aníbal Quijano, "Coloniality and Modernity/Rationality," *Cultural Studies* 21, no. 2 (2007), 168–178.

3. Homi Bhabha, *The Location of Culture* (London: Routledge, 1994), 9.

I found this entry point through two embodied memories that balance on the verge of affective and rational, and both have to do with (re)weaving of words, threads, and eventually, worlds and selves. The first memory similar to Kahraman's *mahaffa* is an *adras* (wild silk) *kurpacha* (mattress), hand-made for me nearly fifty years ago by my grandmother, who also had to sacrifice her older self and identity to survive in the neo-colonial space of the Soviet Uzbekistan. The worn-out mattress that I carried from the Northern Caucasus to Moscow and now to Linköping serves as a security object in my lonely Swedish existence. The second memory is of a lost object from my childhood—a 1970s Russian translation of *Maqamat al Hariri*[4] which we had in our family library and which I remember leafing through as a child. It included replicas of the fascinating 13th-century illustrations of Abu Zayd al-Saruji's adventures, revived and rethought in Kahraman's works.

What captivates me in work after work is how boldly the artist de-automatizes our habitual notions of the beautiful and sublime, personal and communal, self and other, masculine and feminine, how easily she hybridizes and problematizes contemporary (Western by default), ethnic (seen as inferior and outdated), and commercialized multicultural art. Negotiating the extremes of assimilation and nationalist essentialism, Kahraman, while balancing between these different forms of appropriation and silencing, reinvents her creative strategies of resistance again and again.

The artist problematizes performativity, visuality, and perception through a number of all-encompassing leitmotifs interpreted both literally and symbolically. One example is how shredding, puncturing, weaving, and mending alternate in a complex overall act of resistance and eventual re-existence. Similarly to Colombian artist Adolfo Albán-Achinte, who invented the term "re-existence,"[5] Kahraman also performs a disobedient act when she incorporates and reworks the textures, sounds, odors, and colors of her community's and her own personal past. This allows the negated and erased forms of relating to the world to reemerge and trigger a decolonial sensual response of regaining her agency and dignity, designing a whole world out of the pieces of shredded canvases.

Kahraman's work with shredding, puncturing, and weaving seems to be a form of transference that helps her to survive, channeling destructive and even suicidal impulses into healing creative routes. In many ancient cultural traditions, weaving reproduces the empowering ritual of keeping the cosmic order and being responsible for creation and growth. One weaves a

4. *Maqamat al Hariri* is an 11–12th-century classical Middle Eastern literary work combining the picaresque element with indirect moral edification; reflections on poetry, philosophy, and religion; and the perfection of Arabic language and grammar. It was composed by al-Hariri of Basra and made known in the Muslim world through illuminated manuscripts depicting the adventures and journeys of the main character—a dodgy, but well educated, talented and smart Abu Zayd al-Saruji.

5. Adolfo Albán-Achinte, "Artistas indígenas y afrocolombianos: Entre las memorias y las cosmovisiones. Estéticas de la re-existencia," in *Arte y estética en la encrucijada descolonial*, ed. Zulma Palermo (Buenos Aires: Del Siglo, 2009), 83–112.

fabric, a story, a self, a language, a history, a world. Accentuating the act of weaving, Kahraman also draws attention to the creolized nature of migrant and translated identities, cultural and art forms, and multilayered memories. As in Édouard Glissant's famous metaphor, she weaves fabrics out of her opacities and "focuses on the texture of the weave and not on the nature of its components."[6]

There are no pure cultural forms or identities to go back to or assimilate with. Kahraman is free from any primordialist, pure authenticity in her interpretation of Iraqi culture. Her fluid and changeable trans-diaspora is a mode of cultural production[7] and a community of displaced border people for whom eternal transit and unresolved hybridity are a chosen identity. She knows that culture changes together with the people carrying their often tragic experience. But there is no going back to the past. And the past is not peacefully waiting for us to return, as in *Bab el Sheikh* (2013). Kahraman's temporality is nonlinear, multilayered, and non-progressivist. The elements of Iraqi culture and way of life are not marked as the finished past as they interpenetrate and reshuffle with contemporary features, escaping the usual either/or logic. Everything exists simultaneously and does not exclude but rather complements one another in her multi-spatial palimpsests existing in the "unsettled magma between different worlds."[8]

The artist's function then is that of a transmitter, carrier, and translator of collective and personal entangled memories stubbornly resisting the official memory politics. The weaving pattern allows her to overcome the artificial, constructed dichotomy of traditional and modern as she dynamically stitches together and relives the erased and censored past in a constant argument with Western modernity, taking into account the temporal lag and all the experiences of struggle, compromises, losses, and gains that have taken place in her life. The revived memory then becomes a weapon no less powerful (but constructive and regenerating) than the sonic weapon of the American forces that triggered several of Kahraman's works such as *LRAD.1* (2016).

Corporeally reproducing and repeating her own personal or communal traumatic experiences, the artist initiates re-existence. Her extreme depersonalization in the act of scanning and reassembling/re-membering her "self" becomes a survival technique of mocking mimicry, intensified by the interplay of imperial and colonial gazes. *She* is a reservoir and an instrument of corporeal and spatial memories, physically trying on and deciphering different and often conflicting identities such as the American troops and the persecuted local civilians in

6.
Édouard Glissant, *Poetics of Relation* (Ann Arbor, MI: University of Michigan Press, 1997), 190.

7.
Steven Vertovec, "Three Meanings of 'Diaspora,' Exemplified among South Asian Religions," in *Diaspora* 6, no. 3 (1997), 277–299.

8.
Bharati Mukherjee, "A Four-Hundred-Year-Old Woman," in *Critical Fictions: The Politics of Imaginative Writing*, ed. Philomena Mariani (Seattle: Bay Press, 1991), 27.

Kahraman's *Search* (2016) [fig. 12] or *Location of Attacker* (2017) [fig. 8], the executed women in *Three Women Hanging* (2008), or the ghosts of the destroyed houses as in *Bab el Sheikh*.

All the layers that form the open and never finite totality of "I" in Trinh T. Minh-ha's formulation[9] constantly re-emerge in bits and pieces of Kahraman's works. The infinite selves leaking into each other blur the borders between categories, selves, and memories. The "leaking" categories and identities are embodied in multilayered images and objects in Kahraman's works. For example, the *Body Screen* (2013) fuses the idea of the screen as a shield in a traditional Iraqi house, dividing and connecting the public and the private areas, and the screening of the artist's own body with a scanner. Woven into this interplay is also the concept of overseeing and being looked at as a manifestation of power or lack of it, destabilizing the canonical discourse on the male gaze.

The recurrent weaving pattern in Kahraman's works turns into a separate art form, which could be called *métissage*. Glissant and later Françoise Lionnet suggested this expressive concept to describe a weaving of voices that links interpretative practices with the construction of subjectivity.[10] The weaving metaphor materializes in the physical form: a *métissage* as a form of tissage (from tissé—to weave). But *métissage* is also an inherently relational poetics, "non-linear, non-prophetic and woven from arduous patience and incomprehensible detours."[11] Kahraman's *She* is such a *métisse*—a hybrid woman with a Middle Eastern face and a Renaissance-patterned body, who is attempting over and over again to reweave her destiny, to become a Moira of her own fate.

Focusing on the texture of the weave is often a multilayered exercise overloaded with different associations and detours that not many viewers are able to grasp. The weave, redesigning *Her* anew, imitates the traditional pattern of *mahaffa* fan—an instrument helping one to breathe freely—yet at the same time reproduces the shape of the audio-transmitters associated with war and death. It allows *Her* to breathe through the punctured surface yet also resembles a target placed on the victim's vital organs. It looks like a shield against the sonic weapon and like a location of the sonic wound that Kahraman attempts to heal. In this contradictory mixture of impulses concentrated in a particular weaving texture emerges a decolonial act of overcoming and empowerment. This act is embodied in a very special heroine who is a healing yet disturbing projection of Kahraman's self, a receptacle of violence, yet also a corporeal space of revival.

9.
Trinh T. Minh-ha, *Woman, Native, Other: Writing Postcoloniality and Feminism*, 93–94.

10.
Françoise Lionnet, *Postcolonial Representations: Women, Literature, Identity* (Ithaca, NY: Cornell University Press, 1989), 29.

11.
Édouard Glissant, *Le Discours Antillais* (Paris: Seuil, 1981), 251.

12.
Abu Muhammad al-Qasim ibn `Ali al-Hariri, *Maqamat al-Hariri*, ed. `Isa Saba (Beirut, Lebanon: Dar Sadr; Dar Beirut, 1970).

13.
Fernando Ortiz, *Cuban Counterpoint: Tobacco and Sugar*, trans. Harriet de Onís (Durham, NC: Duke University Press, 1995), 98.

She is a trickster figure recurrent in many colonial traditions, a magmatic escaping multiple personas. Kahraman's play on *Maqamat*[12] (*Kachakchi* [2015] [fig. 11])—a medieval Middle Eastern picaresque genre, which in fact preceded its better-known European forms by several centuries—acquires additional meanings in this context. It is a form of transculturation[13] and an act of remaking the itinerant philosopher, poet, and rogue Abu Zayd al-Saruji in a female form. Just as Abu Zayd easily moved from Iraq to Egypt and from the Caucasus to Yemen, *She* is also a compulsory cosmopolitan migrant who mimics the host environment yet makes fun of it and manipulates it at the same time, always escaping definition and appropriation, always hiding one more layer in her infinite set of identifications.

Kahraman decolonizes many elements of classical and contemporary western aesthetics by transforming and creolizing their established and habitual genres and enriching them with new meanings. For example, the recognizable Renaissance ideal of a beautiful female body and the use of *sfumato* technique are disrupted by the unfocused, absent, or even blind gazes of her serialized protagonists, by their unbound, ghost-like, and free way of floating over the surface rather than standing firmly on the ground or being surrounded by a landscape. This composition is the opposite of the Renaissance realistic aesthetic. Kahraman even decolonizes the typical Renaissance material—linen canvas used for oil painting—by shredding and reweaving it anew. Once again, it is the texture of the rich transcultural weave that is more important than the original ingredients, be they Renaissance, Middle Eastern, or Japanese.

Kahraman also remakes performance as a body-centered art form into a longer processual negotiation of private and public acts. She separates the main elements of performance as a contemporary genre in a temporal, spatial, and communicative sense. Performance usually contains four basic elements—time, space, the artist's body, and the relation of the audience and the artist. Kahraman complicates this structure by combining the first three elements in a private metonymic recital and its photo-documentation, not shown to the audience, whereas the resulting paintings or installations bring us back to the more traditional metaphoric forms of representation as a set of objects in a museum environment. Contrary to body-art where the body replaces the canvas, Kahraman replaces her body with a canvas, with wood, with skin, and with other materials undergoing specific destroying and remaking manipulations. Yet the history of the emergence of these resulting objects is not hidden or erased. Its traces are palpable, leaking, seen, and felt in the uneven and scarred textures of Kahraman's works, reproducing the "geography of pain" and the woman's body as a site of conflict.[14]

Deconstructing her body to an almost molecular level, humbly taking it to a set of elements in which it is impossible to detect anymore the human "self," Kahraman then reassembles *Her* anew in fascinating works incorporating her body scans and superimposing them onto various geometric figures representing the key motives of her work, as in *Decagram 2* (2013) and *Icosahedron* (2013). The ideally harmonious Platonic figure, symbolizing the world, seems to be decorated with Islamic ornaments, whereas in reality the presumably ancient ornaments turn out to be the super high-tech images of the scanned parts of Kahraman's body. The viewer is expected to perceive such works relationally—as an image of the disassembled body, as a multiple self, and as an intimate portrait of the author—drawn on the "body" of the world and putting both the world and the self back together. Through trauma, humiliation, fear, loss, and survival, Kahraman reweaves her self and her world anew, turning resistance into re-existence and a life-asserting and liberating promise of the future.

14. Françoise Lionnet, "Geographies of Pain: Captive Bodies and Violent Acts in the Fictions of Myriam Warner-Vieyra, Gayl Jones, and Bessie Head," *Callaloo* 16, no. 1 (Winter 1993), 132–152.

Dismemberment

Sinan Antoon

تفكّك

سنان أنطون

The body, or a voice impersonating it, said:
          Go! As of now, you are all free

The eyes flew far away, joining flocks
of other eyes
          which had filled the sky

قال الجسد أو صوت يتقمصه:
اذهبوا أنتم منذ الساعة أحرار.

almost blocking the sunlight

طارت العينان بعيداً والتحقتا بسرب العيون التي ملأت السماء

وتكاد تحجب ضوء الشمس

قال الجسد، أو صوتٌ يَنْتحلُ هويته:
إذهبوا، فأنتم، منذ الساعة، أحرار.

طارت العينان بعيداً، والتحقتا بأسراب العيون التي ملأت السماء

وكادت تحجب ضوء الشمس

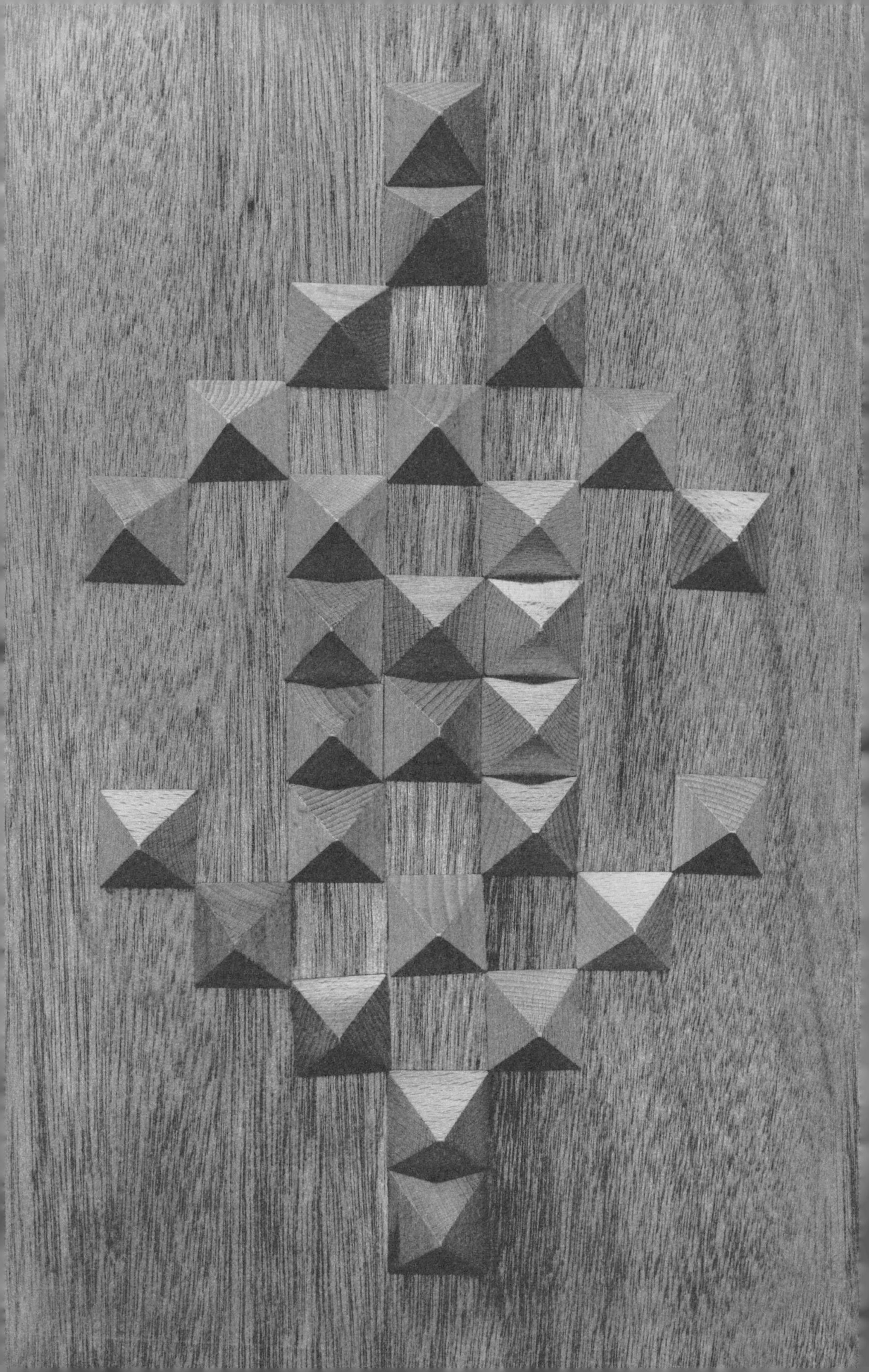

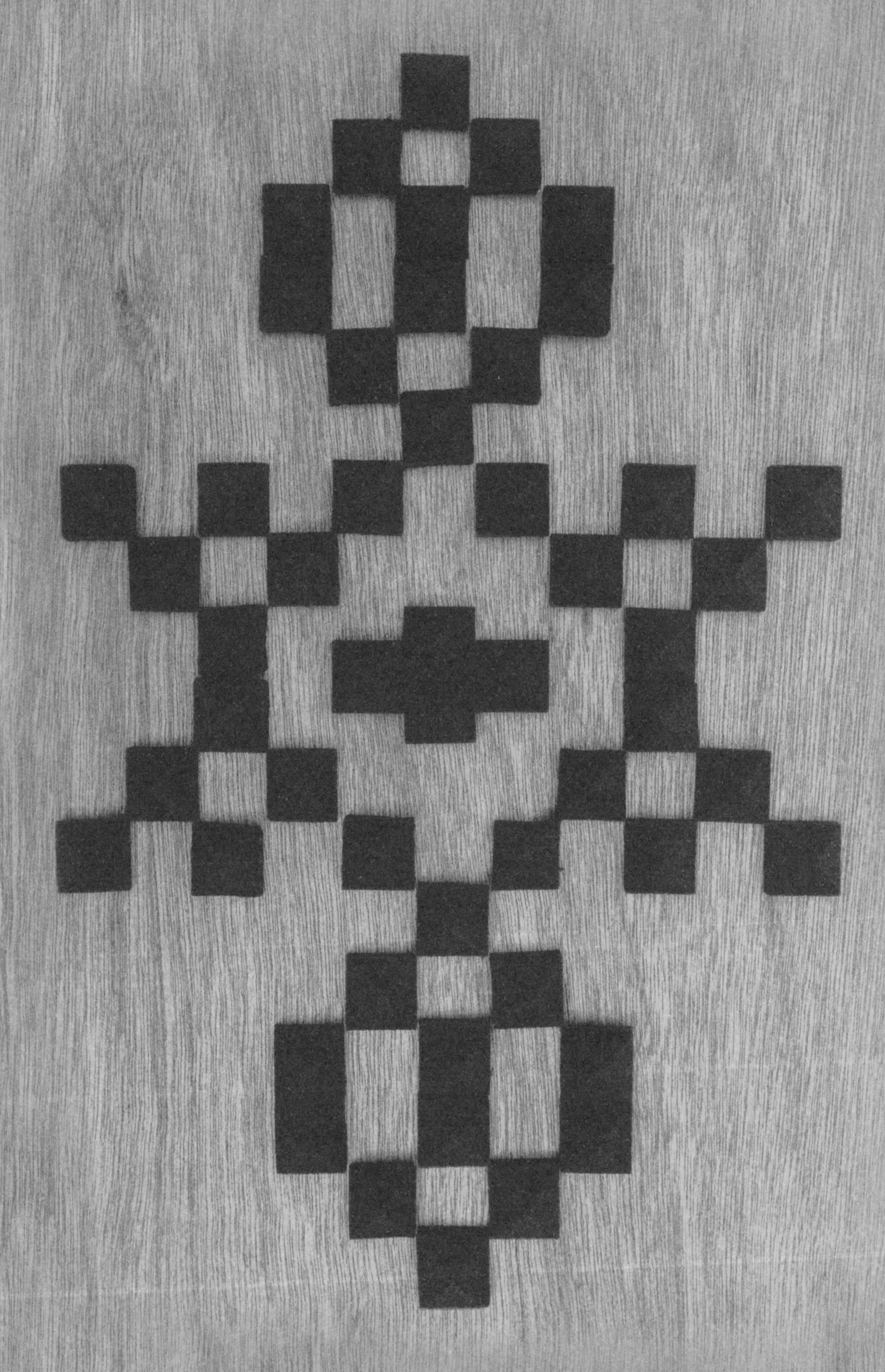

The lips parted company without a farewell

One searched for a new face
the other for a lip that would listen
to its complaints

الشفتان افترقتا بلا وداع

واحدة بحثت عن وجه جديد
والأخرى عن شفة تصغي إلى شكواها

الشفتان افترقتا بلا وداع

واحدة تبحث عن وجه جديد
والأخرى عن شفة تصغي إلى شكواها

The tired tongue sought a mute man's mouth
to rest in

The hands clapped and waved to
each other
as they went away.

أخذ اللسان المتعب يفتّش عن فم رجل أخرس يرتاح فيه
تصفّق الأيادي ثمّ تلوّح لبعضها البعض وهي تبتعد

بدت الساق اليمنى خائفة ومتردّدة ثمّ سارعت لتلحق بالساق اليسرى
سقط الأنف على الأرض. . . وهكذا.

The right leg appeared to be frightened
and hesitant,

then it rushed to catch up with the left leg
The nose fell on the ground. . . and so on.

أخذ اللسان المتعب يفتّش عن فم رجل أخرس يرتاح فيه
صفّقت اليدان، ثمّ لوّحتا لبعضهما البعض وهما تبتعدان

بدت الساق اليمنى خائفة ومتردّدة، ثم سارعت لتلحق بالأخرى
سقط الأنف على الأرض. . . وهكذا.

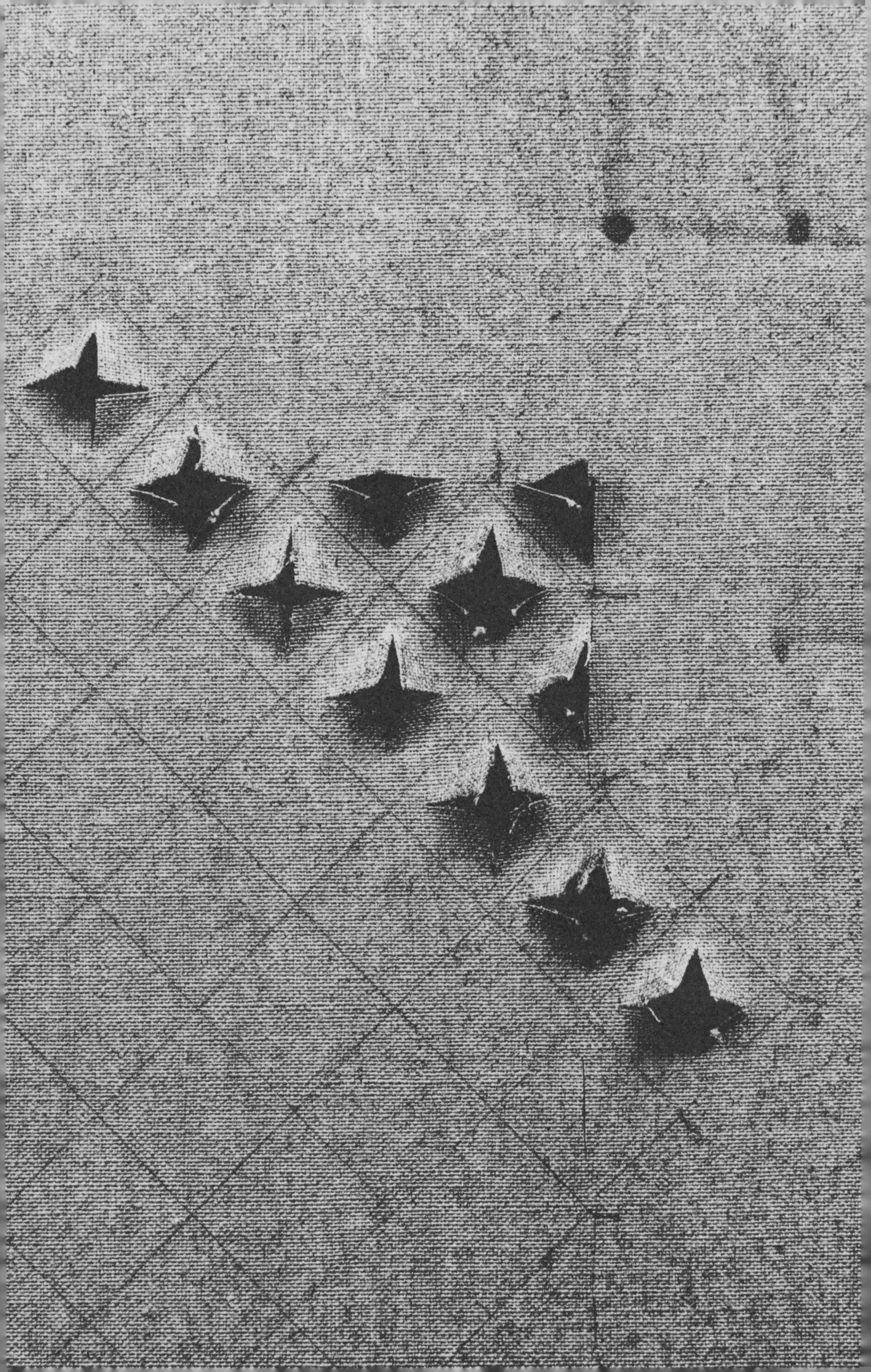

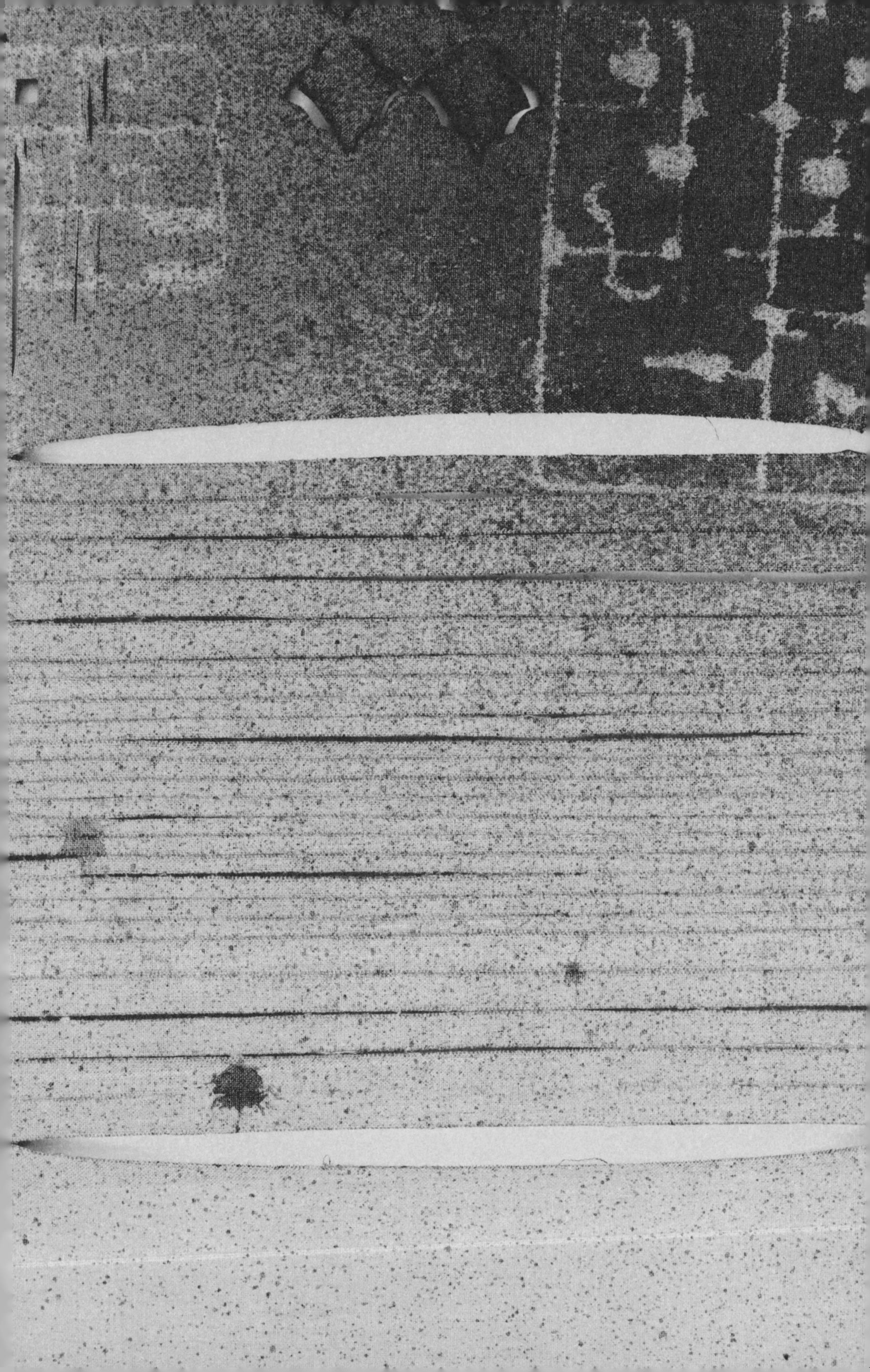

As for the heart, it kept beating

ألخ لقفة بلقاا لةأ

alone

until a lost foot crushed it

أليه م د
وللغاا يف ةتهاث ولة متسعدى رحته نخبني

أمّا القلب فقد ظل

،وحيداً
ينبض حتى دعسته قدم تائهة في الظلام

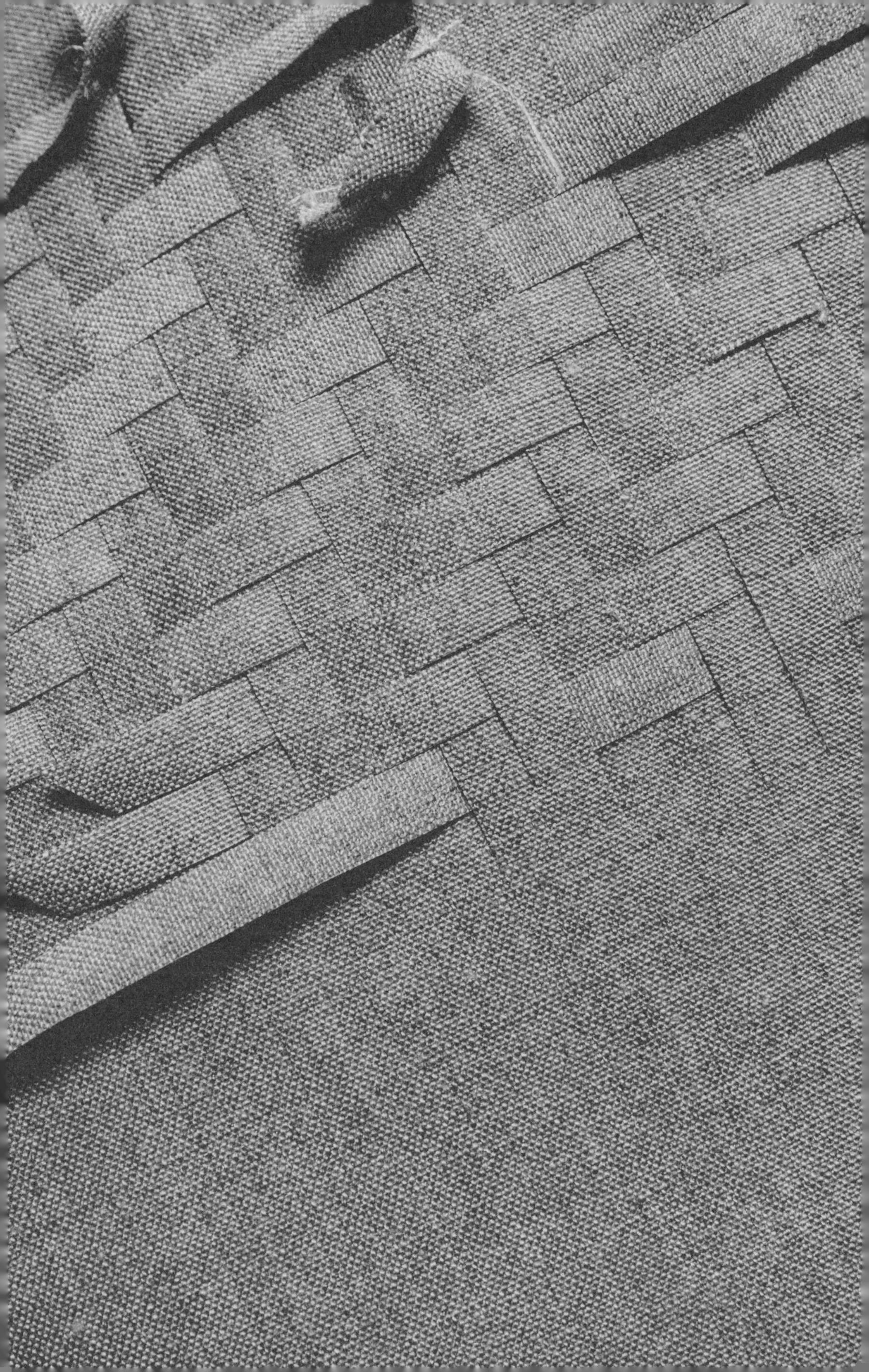

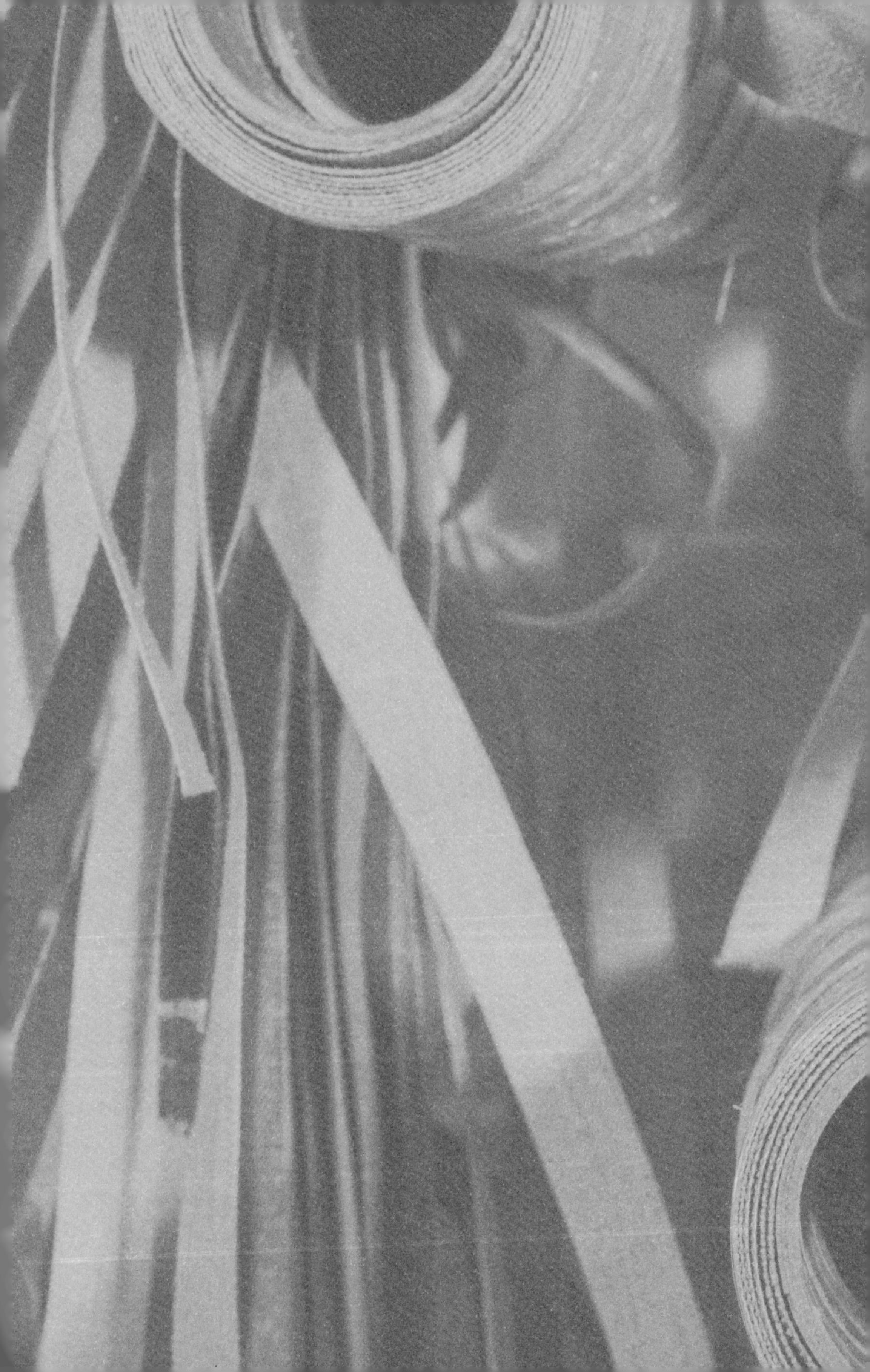